Constitution ILLUSTRATED

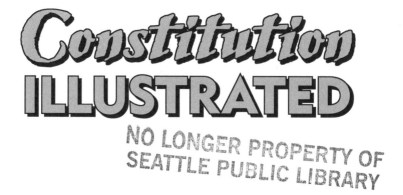

R. SIKORYAK

DRAWN & QUARTERLY

Coloring assistance: Brian Michael Weaver

Thanks to Peggy Burns, Tom Devlin, Tracy Hurren, and everyone at D+Q; Joe Sikoryak, Steve Sikoryak, Steve Gross, and Brian Michael Weaver. Extra special thanks to Kriota, for everything, always.

The Constitution is presented unabridged and reflects the spelling, punctuation, and capitalization of the original document.

drawnandquarterly.com
rsikoryak.com

ISBN 978-1-77046-396-7
First edition: August 2020
Printed in Canada
10 9 8 7 6 5 4 3 2 1

Cataloguing data available from Library and Archives Canada

Published in the USA by Drawn & Quarterly, a client publisher of Farrar, Straus and Giroux; Published in Canada by Drawn & Quarterly, a client publisher of Raincoast Books; Published in the United Kingdom by Drawn & Quarterly, a client publisher of Publishers Group UK

Contents

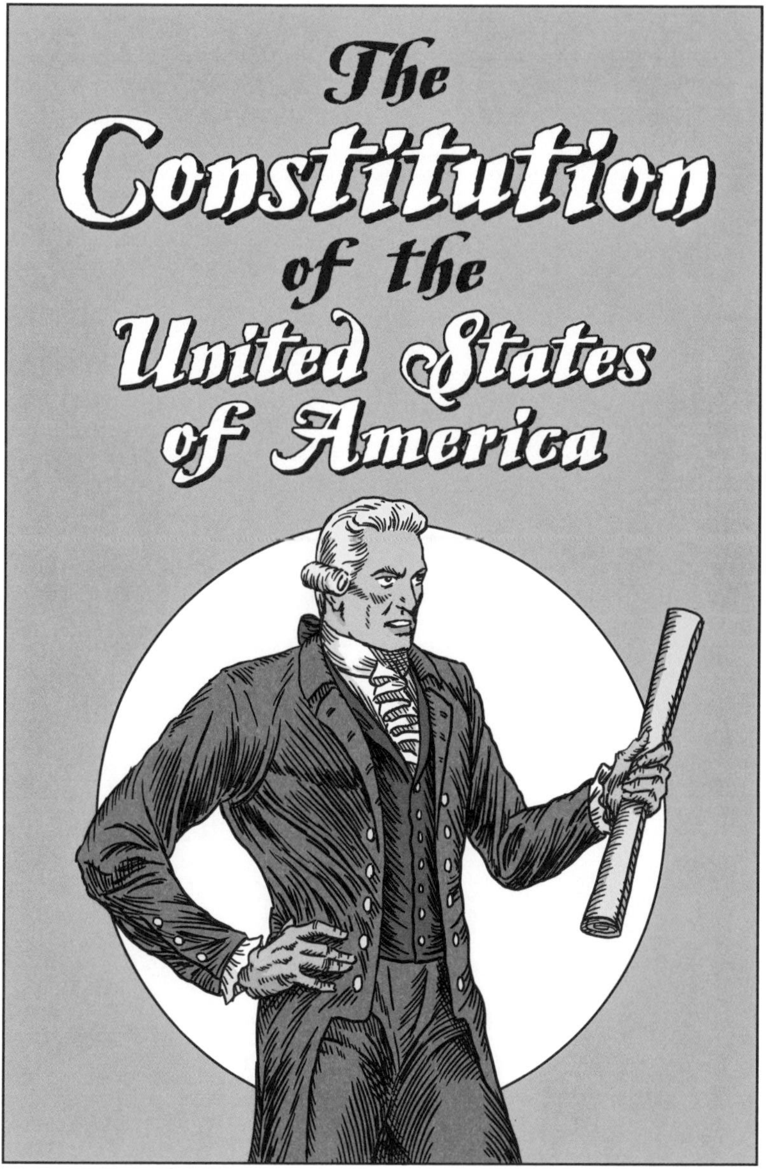
The Constitution of the United States of America

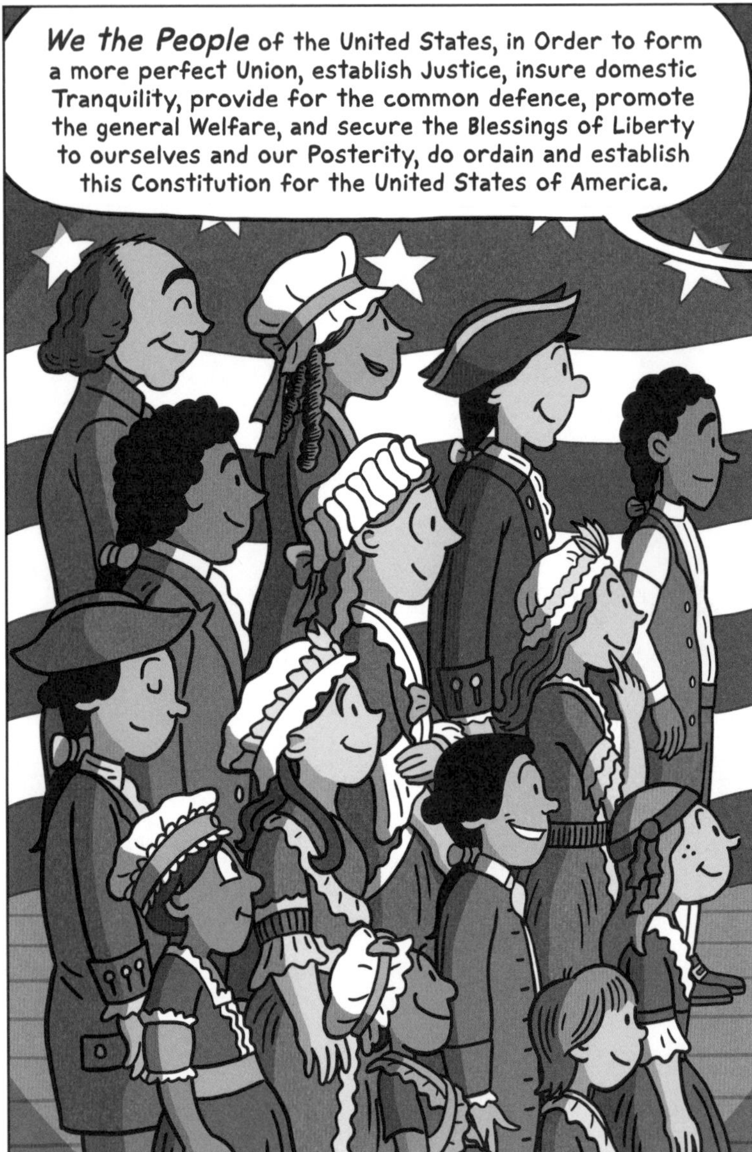
We the People of the United States, in Order to form a more perfect Union, establish Justice, insure domestic Tranquility, provide for the common defence, promote the general Welfare, and secure the Blessings of Liberty to ourselves and our Posterity, do ordain and establish this Constitution for the United States of America.

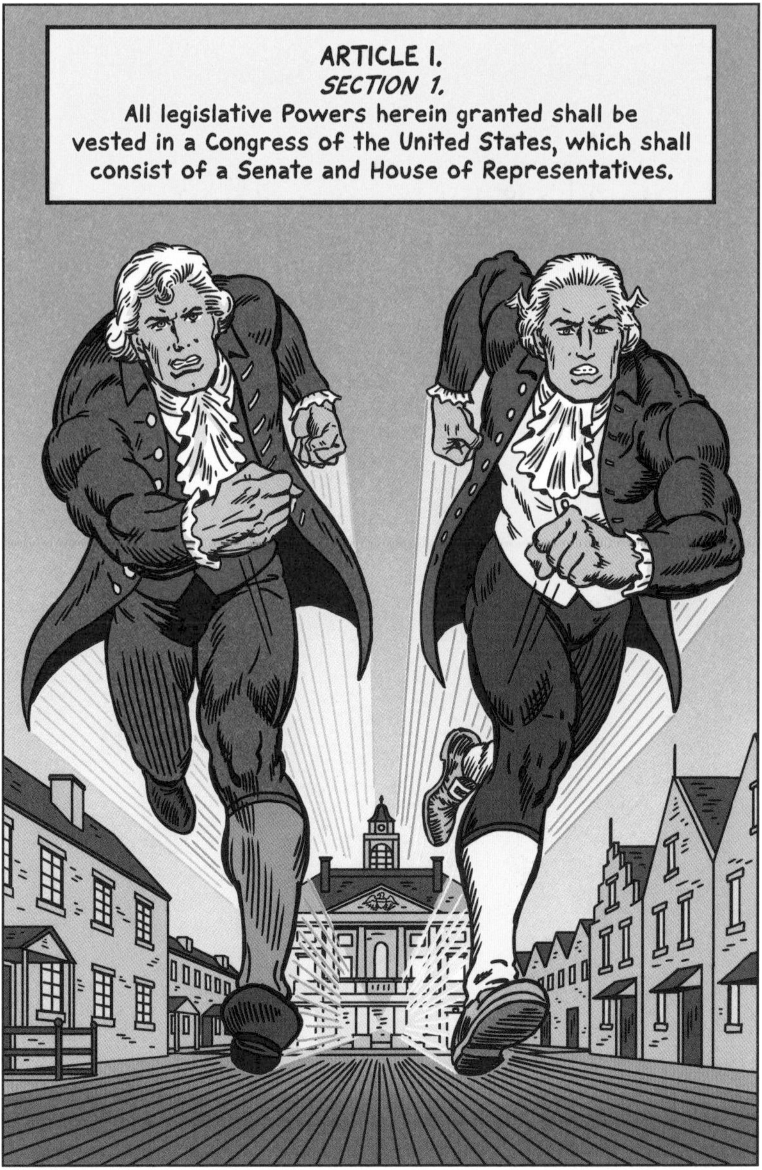
ARTICLE I.
SECTION 1.
All legislative Powers herein granted shall be vested in a Congress of the United States, which shall consist of a Senate and House of Representatives.

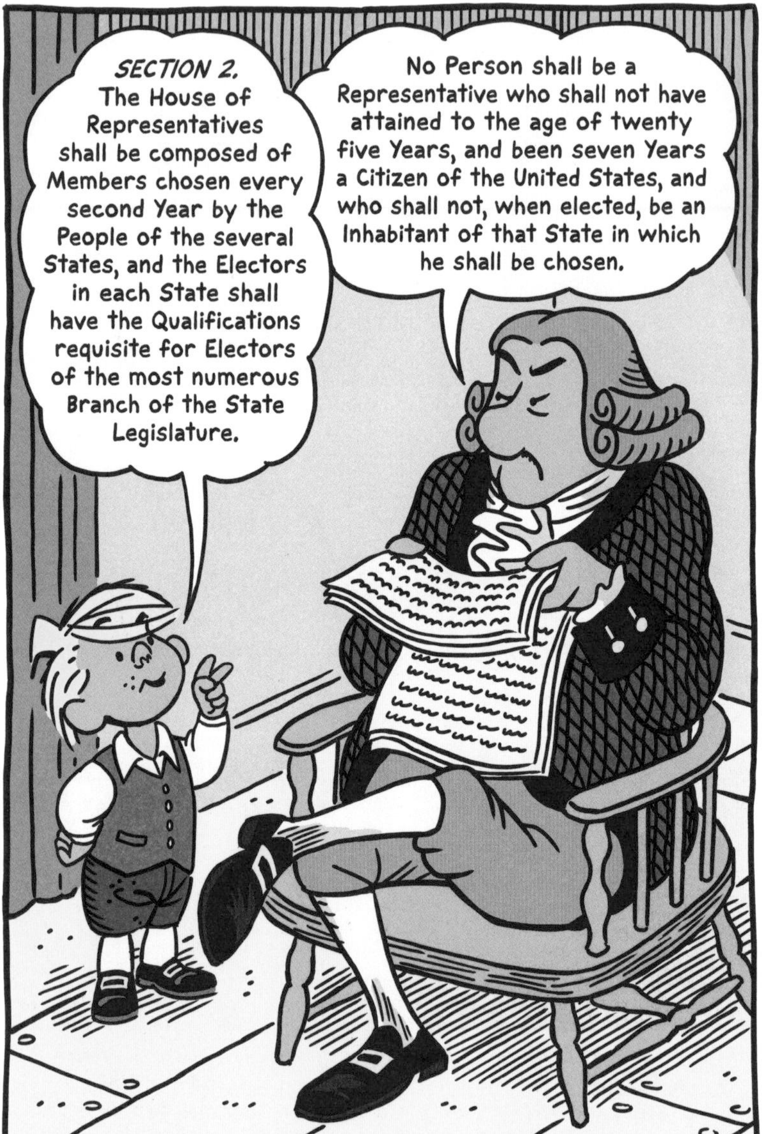
SECTION 2. The House of Representatives shall be composed of Members chosen every second Year by the People of the several States, and the Electors in each State shall have the Qualifications requisite for Electors of the most numerous Branch of the State Legislature.
No Person shall be a Representative who shall not have attained to the age of twenty five Years, and been seven Years a Citizen of the United States, and who shall not, when elected, be an Inhabitant of that State in which he shall be chosen.

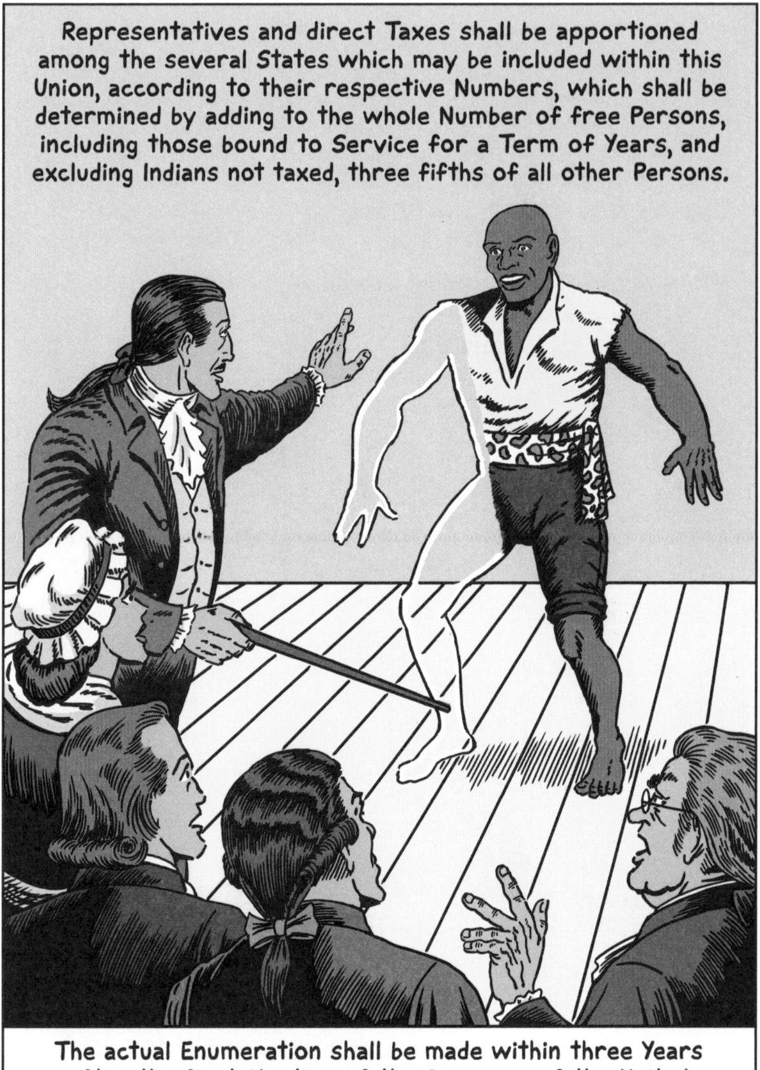
Representatives and direct Taxes shall be apportioned among the several States which may be included within this Union, according to their respective Numbers, which shall be determined by adding to the whole Number of free Persons, including those bound to Service for a Term of Years, and excluding Indians not taxed, three fifths of all other Persons.
The actual Enumeration shall be made within three Years after the first Meeting of the Congress of the United States, and within every subsequent Term of ten Years, in such Manner as they shall by Law direct.

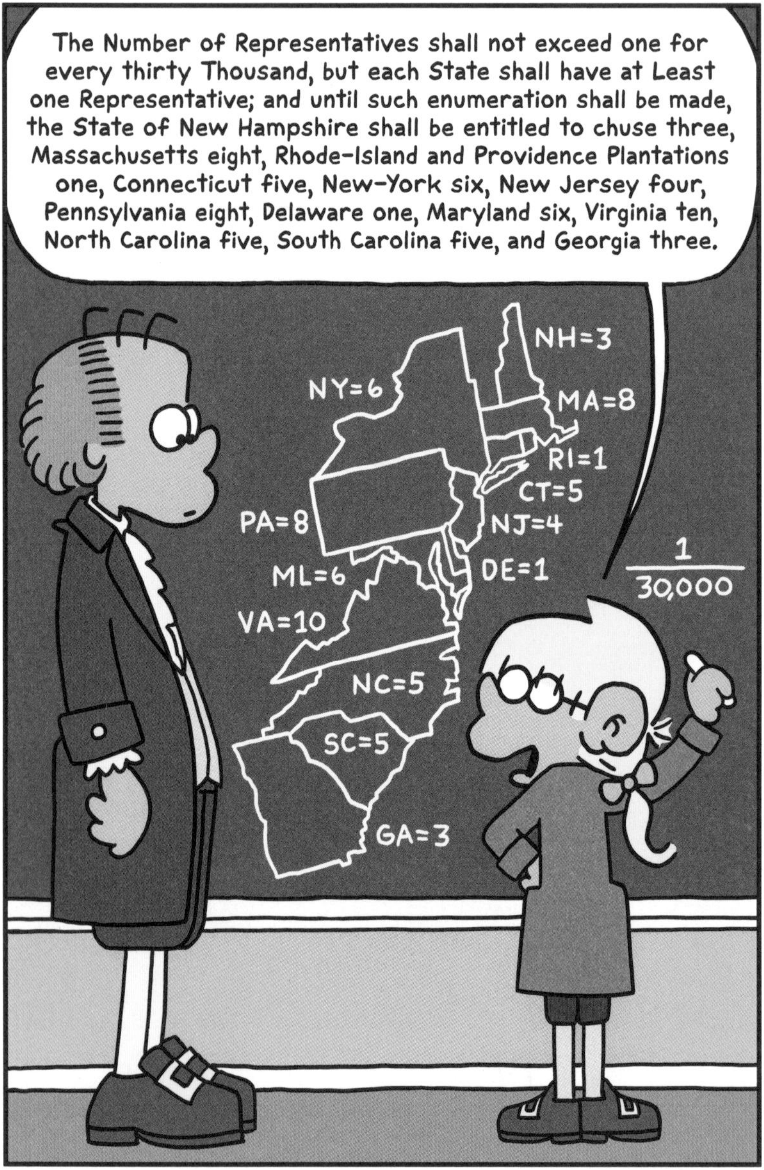
The Number of Representatives shall not exceed one for every thirty Thousand, but each State shall have at Least one Representative; and until such enumeration shall be made, the State of New Hampshire shall be entitled to chuse three, Massachusetts eight, Rhode-Island and Providence Plantations one, Connecticut five, New-York six, New Jersey four, Pennsylvania eight, Delaware one, Maryland six, Virginia ten, North Carolina five, South Carolina five, and Georgia three.
NH=3
NY=6
MA=8
RI=1
CT=5
PA=8
NJ=4
ML=6
DE=1
1/30,000
VA=10
NC=5
SC=5
GA=3

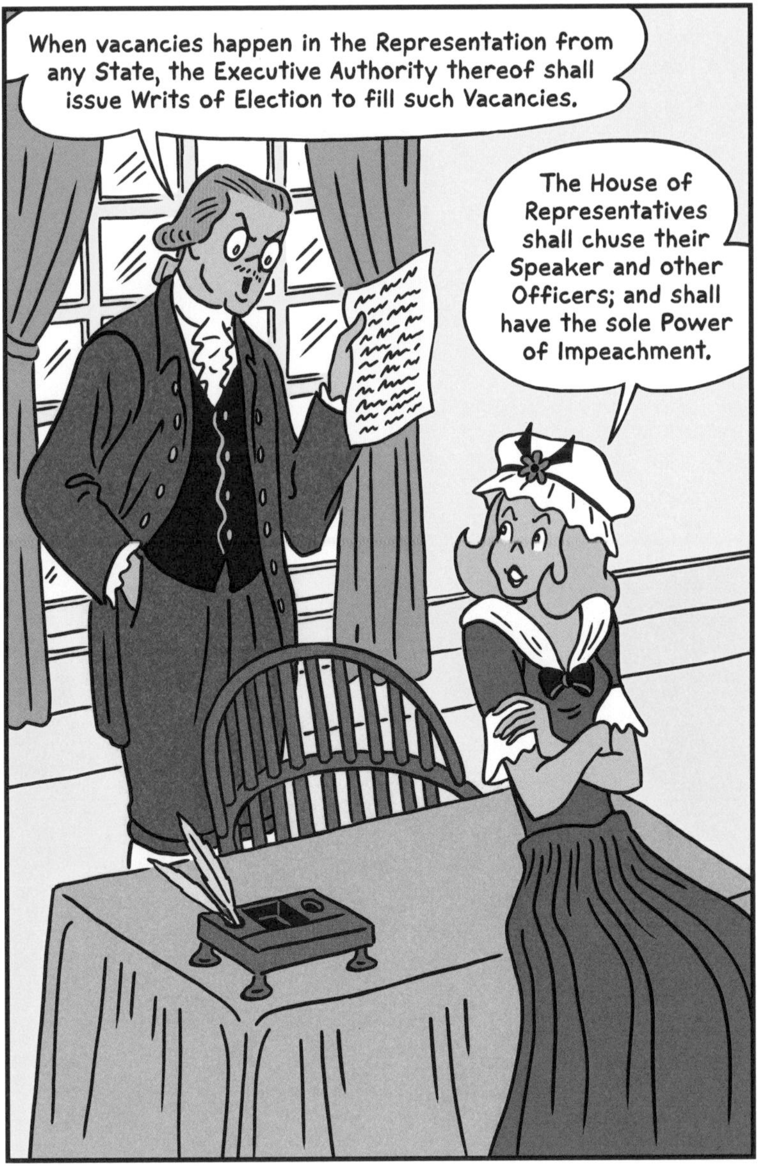
When vacancies happen in the Representation from any State, the Executive Authority thereof shall issue Writs of Election to fill such Vacancies.
The House of Representatives shall chuse their Speaker and other Officers; and shall have the sole Power of Impeachment.

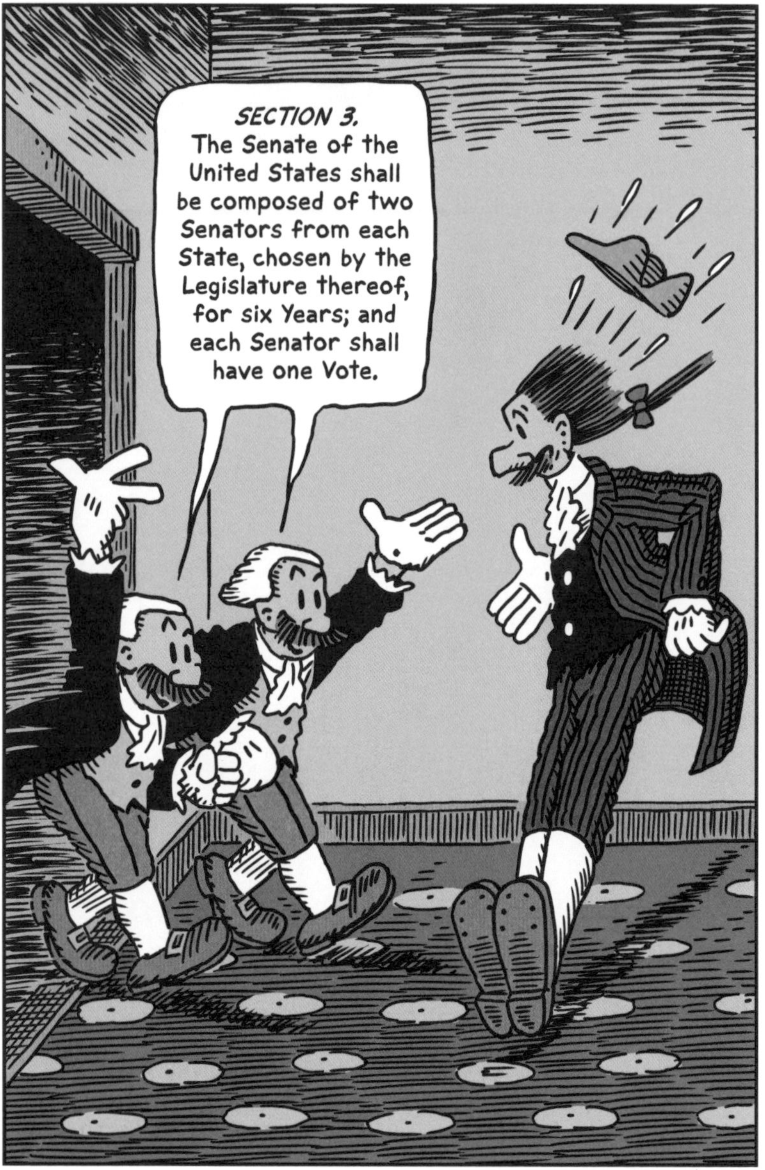
SECTION 3.
The Senate of the United States shall be composed of two Senators from each State, chosen by the Legislature thereof, for six Years; and each Senator shall have one Vote.

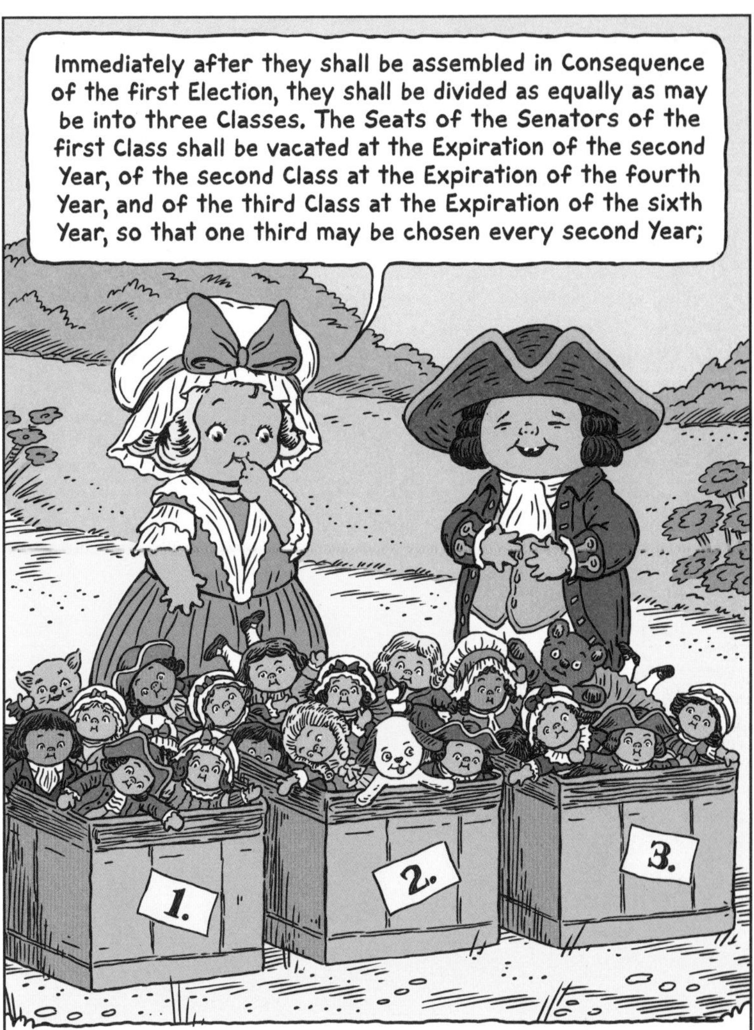
Immediately after they shall be assembled in Consequence of the first Election, they shall be divided as equally as may be into three Classes. The Seats of the Senators of the first Class shall be vacated at the Expiration of the second Year, of the second Class at the Expiration of the fourth Year, and of the third Class at the Expiration of the sixth Year, so that one third may be chosen every second Year;
1.
2.
3.

and if Vacancies happen by Resignation, or otherwise, during the Recess of the Legislature of any State, the Executive thereof may make temporary Appointments until the next Meeting of the Legislature, which shall then fill such Vacancies.

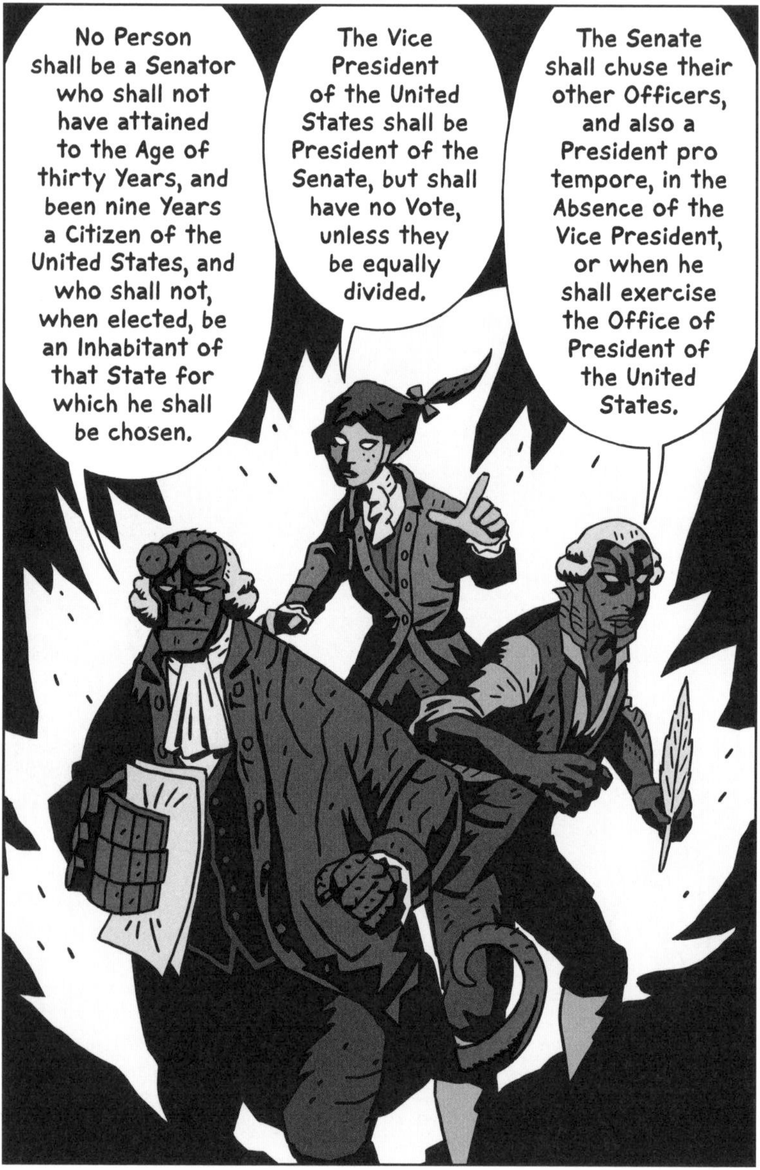
No Person shall be a Senator who shall not have attained to the Age of thirty Years, and been nine Years a Citizen of the United States, and who shall not, when elected, be an Inhabitant of that State for which he shall be chosen.
The Vice President of the United States shall be President of the Senate, but shall have no Vote, unless they be equally divided.
The Senate shall chuse their other Officers, and also a President pro tempore, in the Absence of the Vice President, or when he shall exercise the Office of President of the United States.

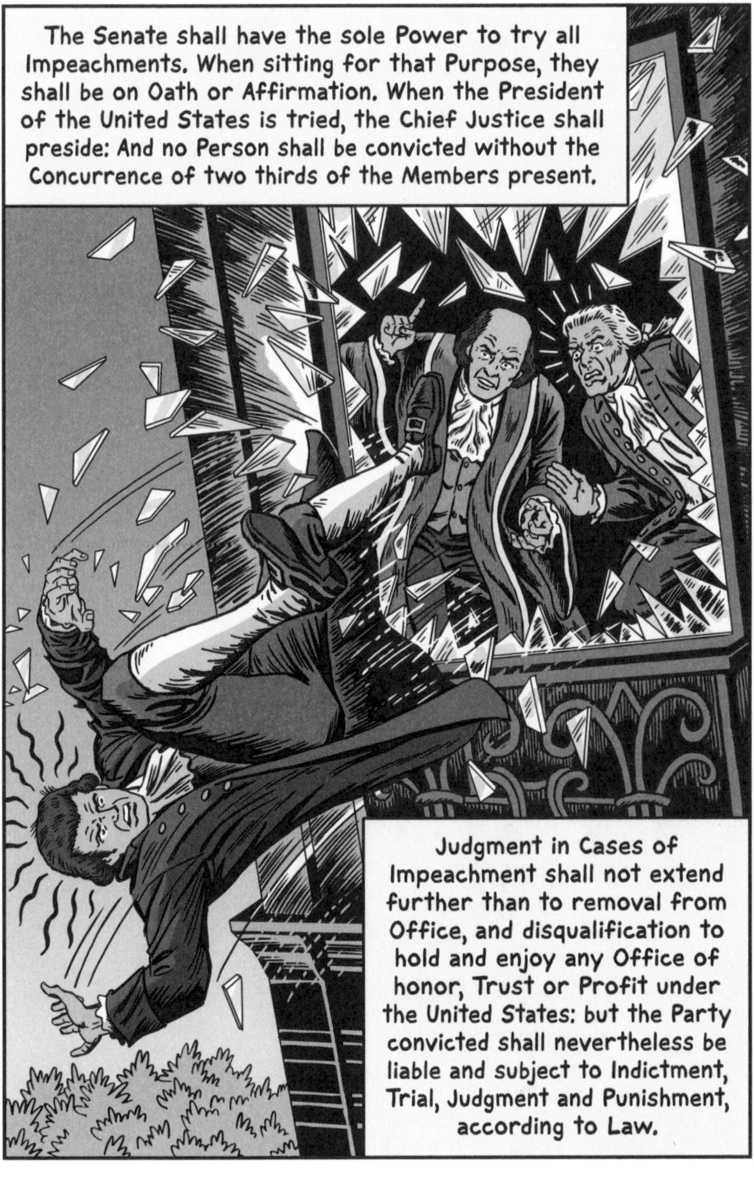
The Senate shall have the sole Power to try all Impeachments. When sitting for that Purpose, they shall be on Oath or Affirmation. When the President of the United States is tried, the Chief Justice shall preside: And no Person shall be convicted without the Concurrence of two thirds of the Members present.
Judgment in Cases of Impeachment shall not extend further than to removal from Office, and disqualification to hold and enjoy any Office of honor, Trust or Profit under the United States: but the Party convicted shall nevertheless be liable and subject to Indictment, Trial, Judgment and Punishment, according to Law.

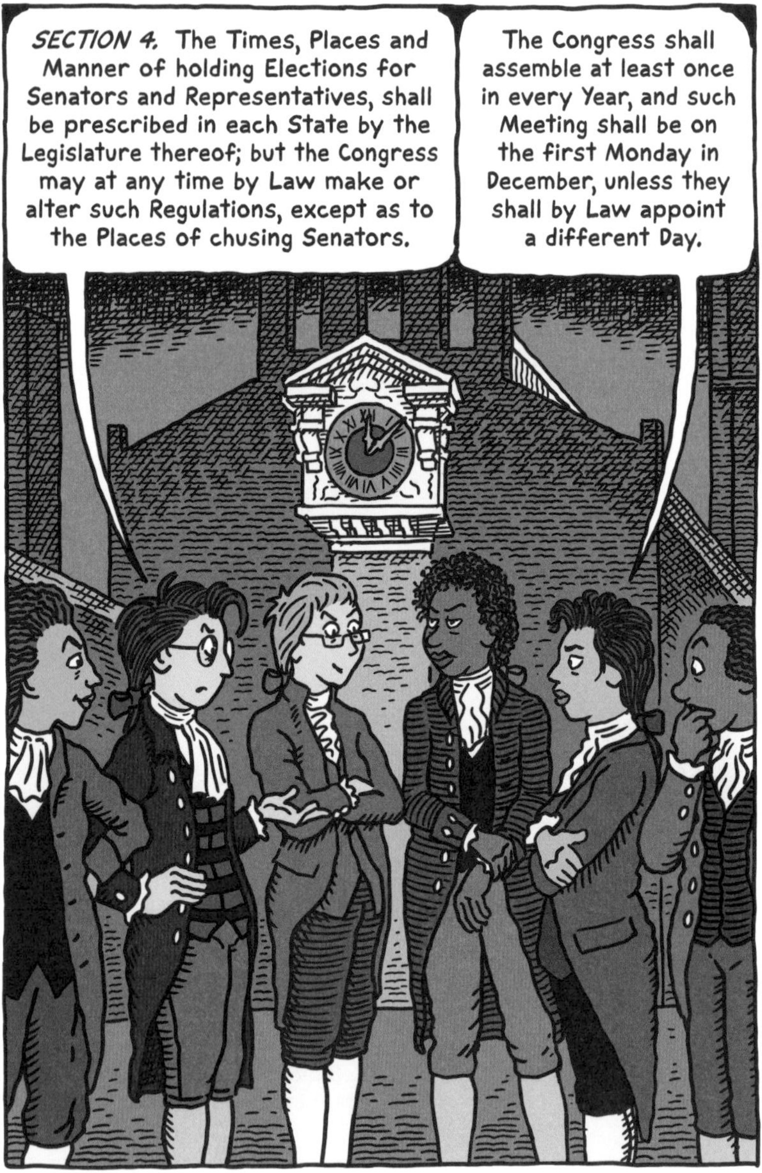
SECTION 4. The Times, Places and Manner of holding Elections for Senators and Representatives, shall be prescribed in each State by the Legislature thereof; but the Congress may at any time by Law make or alter such Regulations, except as to the Places of chusing Senators.
The Congress shall assemble at least once in every Year, and such Meeting shall be on the first Monday in December, unless they shall by Law appoint a different Day.

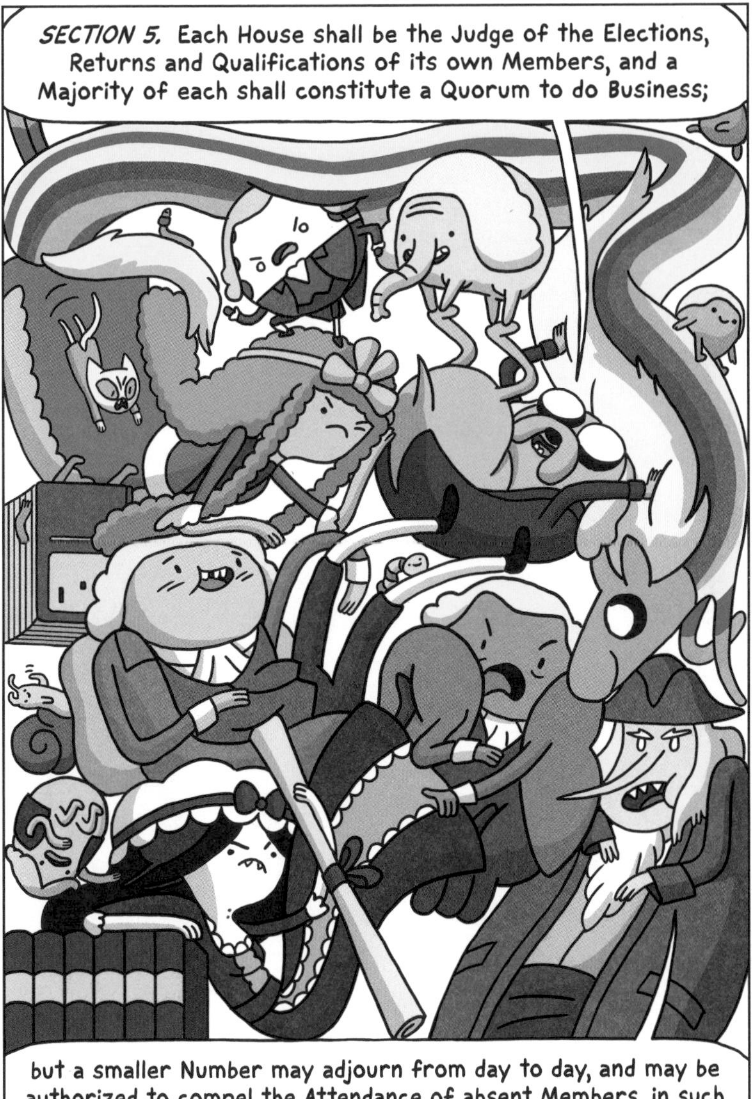
SECTION 5. Each House shall be the Judge of the Elections, Returns and Qualifications of its own Members, and a Majority of each shall constitute a Quorum to do Business;
but a smaller Number may adjourn from day to day, and may be authorized to compel the Attendance of absent Members, in such Manner, and under such Penalties as each House may provide.

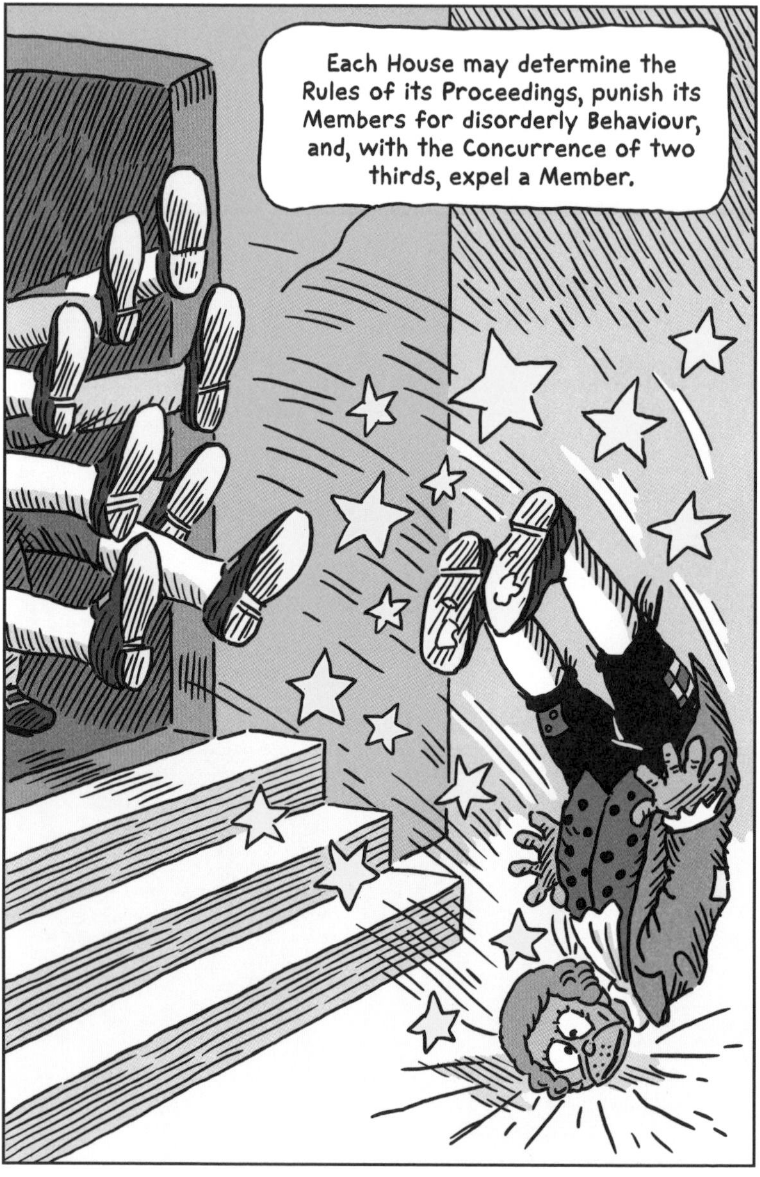
Each House may determine the Rules of its Proceedings, punish its Members for disorderly Behaviour, and, with the Concurrence of two thirds, expel a Member.

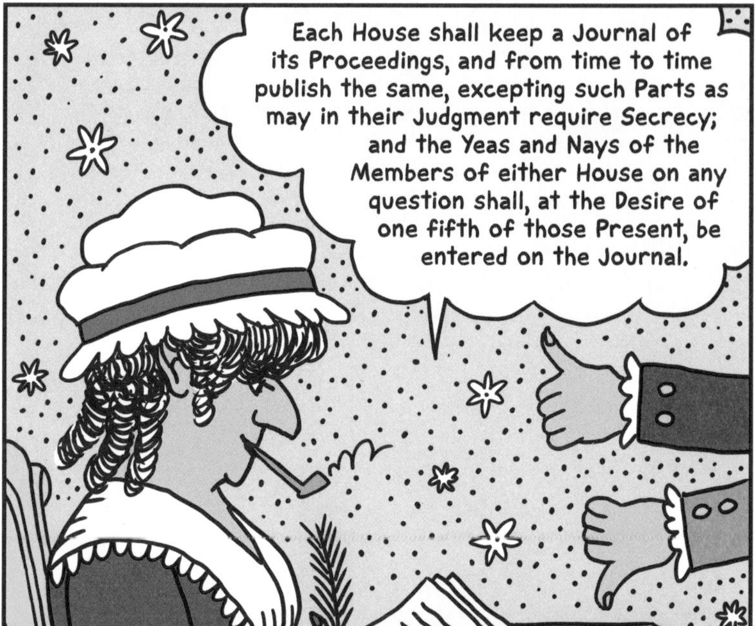
Each House shall keep a Journal of its Proceedings, and from time to time publish the same, excepting such Parts as may in their Judgment require Secrecy; and the Yeas and Nays of the Members of either House on any question shall, at the Desire of one fifth of those Present, be entered on the Journal.

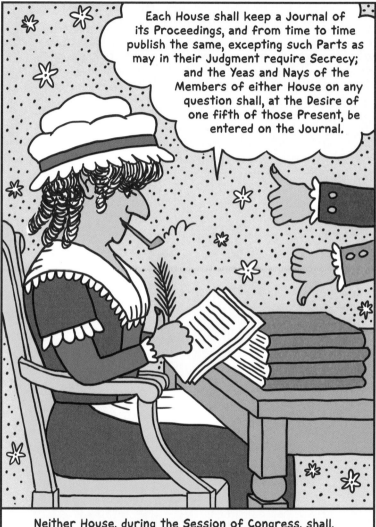

Neither House, during the Session of Congress, shall, without the Consent of the other, adjourn for more than three days, nor to any other Place than that in which the two Houses shall be sitting.

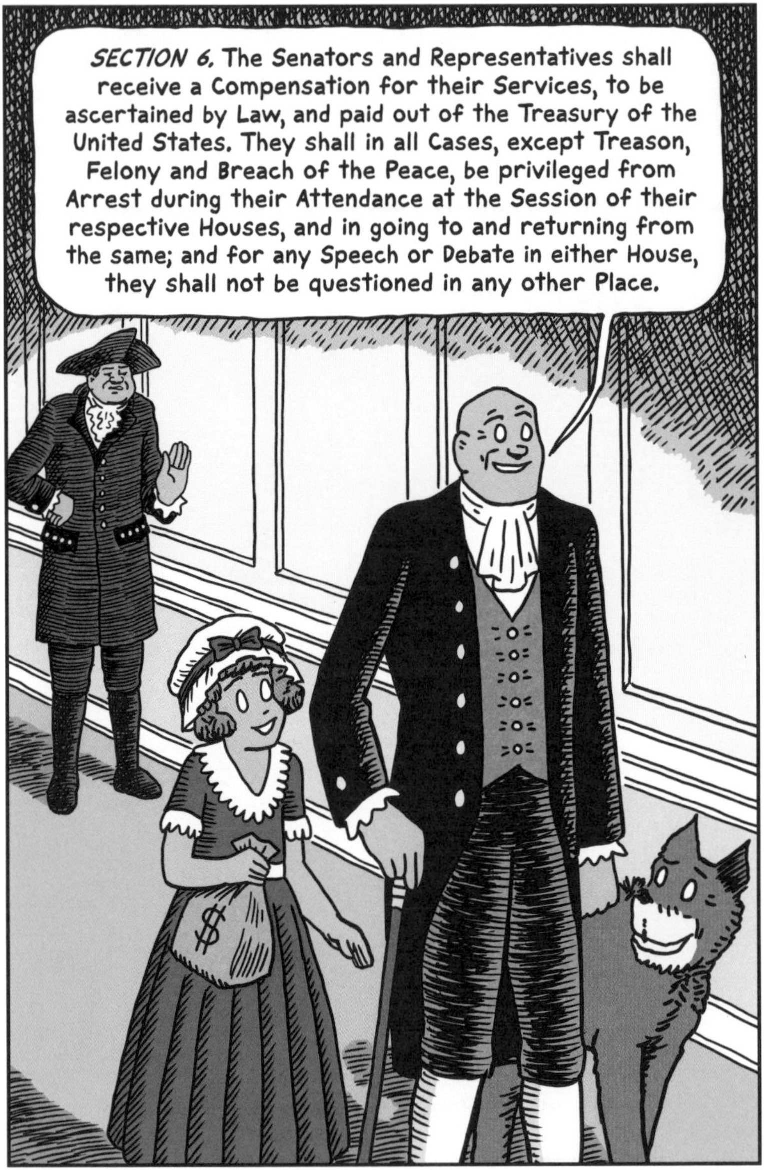
SECTION 6. The Senators and Representatives shall receive a Compensation for their Services, to be ascertained by Law, and paid out of the Treasury of the United States. They shall in all Cases, except Treason, Felony and Breach of the Peace, be privileged from Arrest during their Attendance at the Session of their respective Houses, and in going to and returning from the same; and for any Speech or Debate in either House, they shall not be questioned in any other Place.
$

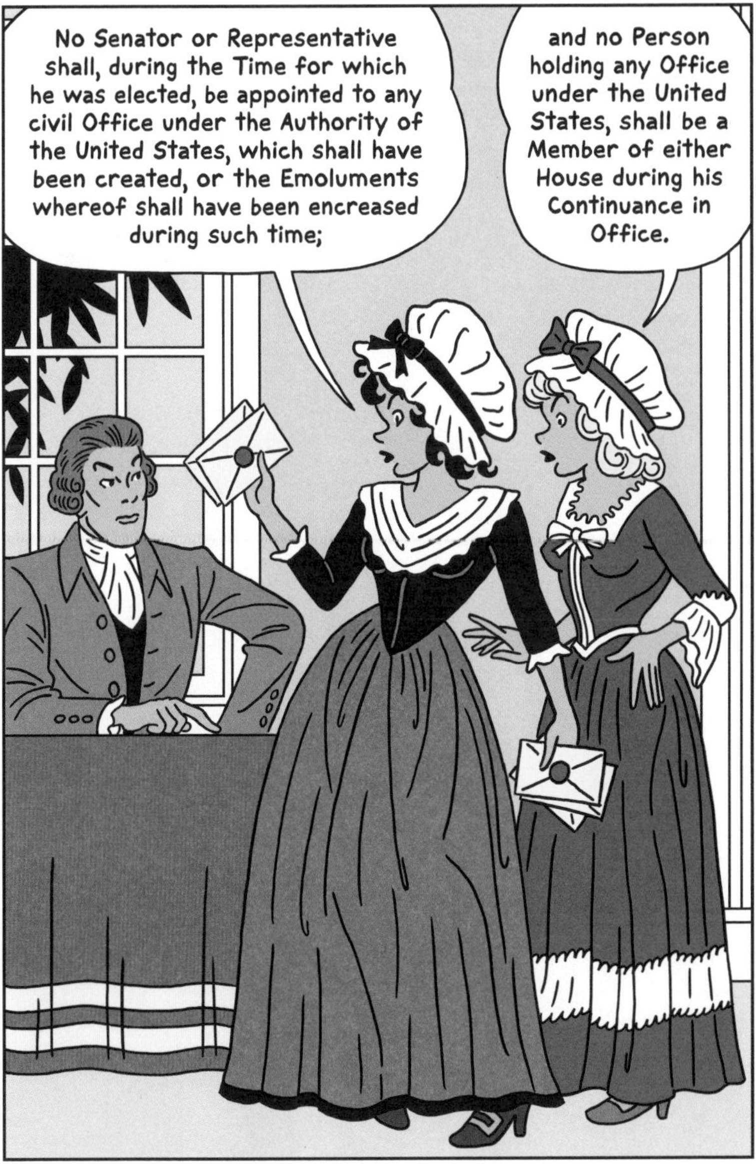
No Senator or Representative shall, during the Time for which he was elected, be appointed to any civil Office under the Authority of the United States, which shall have been created, or the Emoluments whereof shall have been encreased during such time;
and no Person holding any Office under the United States, shall be a Member of either House during his Continuance in Office.

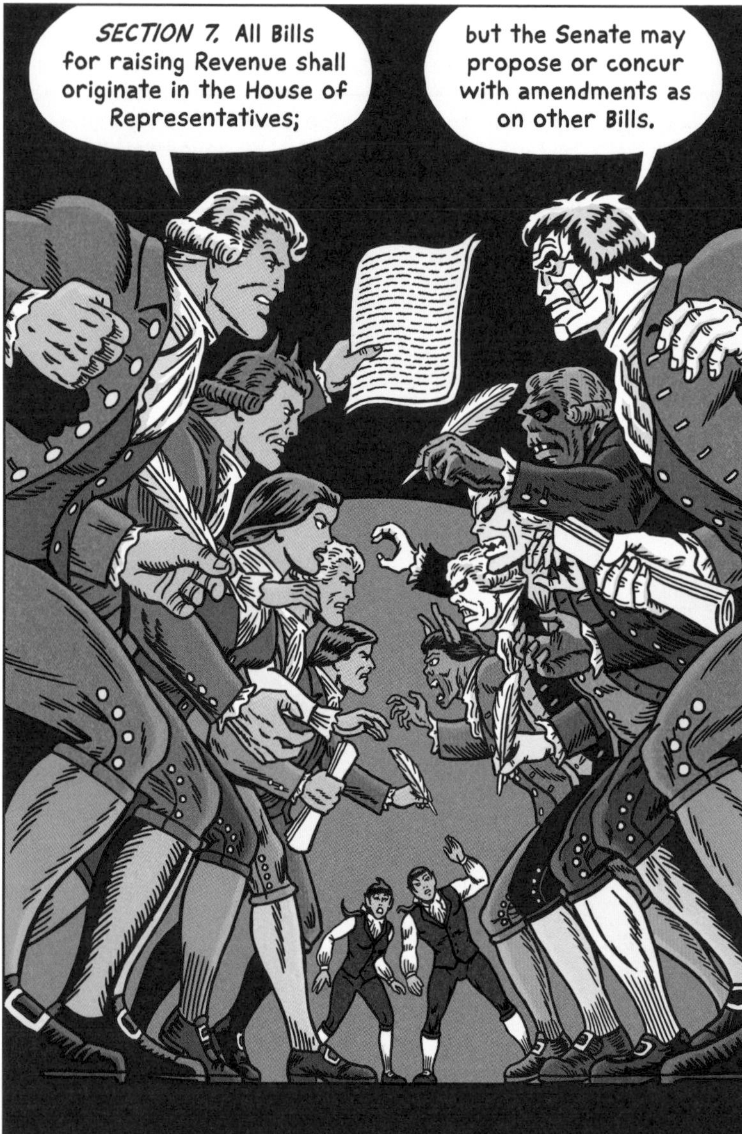
SECTION 7. All Bills for raising Revenue shall originate in the House of Representatives;
but the Senate may propose or concur with amendments as on other Bills.

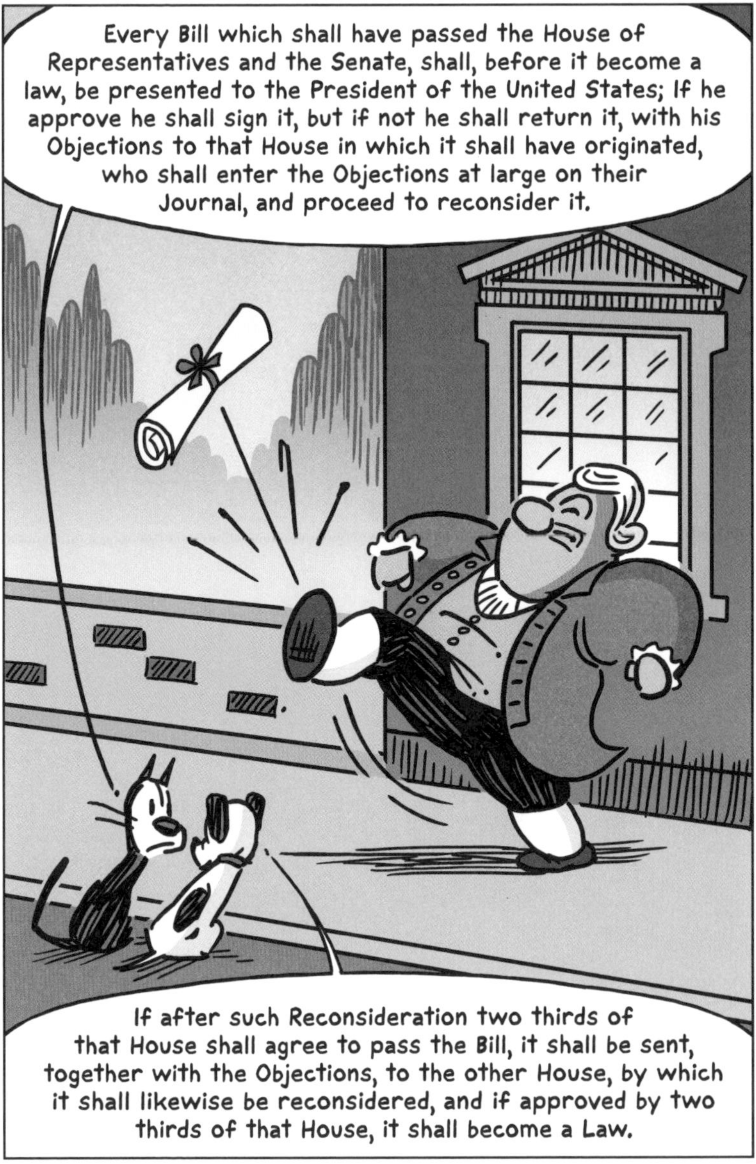
Every Bill which shall have passed the House of Representatives and the Senate, shall, before it become a law, be presented to the President of the United States; If he approve he shall sign it, but if not he shall return it, with his Objections to that House in which it shall have originated, who shall enter the Objections at large on their Journal, and proceed to reconsider it.
If after such Reconsideration two thirds of that House shall agree to pass the Bill, it shall be sent, together with the Objections, to the other House, by which it shall likewise be reconsidered, and if approved by two thirds of that House, it shall become a Law.

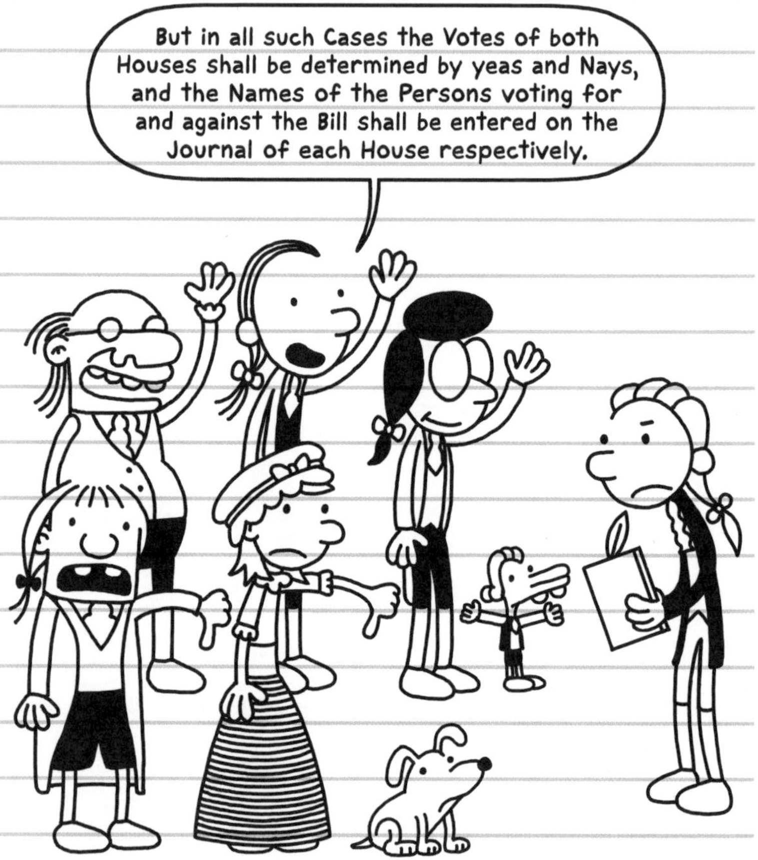
But in all such Cases the Votes of both Houses shall be determined by yeas and Nays, and the Names of the Persons voting for and against the Bill shall be entered on the Journal of each House respectively.

If any Bill shall not be returned by the President within ten Days (Sundays excepted) after it shall have been presented to him, the Same shall be a Law, in like Manner as if he had signed it, unless the Congress by their Adjournment prevent its Return, in which Case it shall not be a Law.

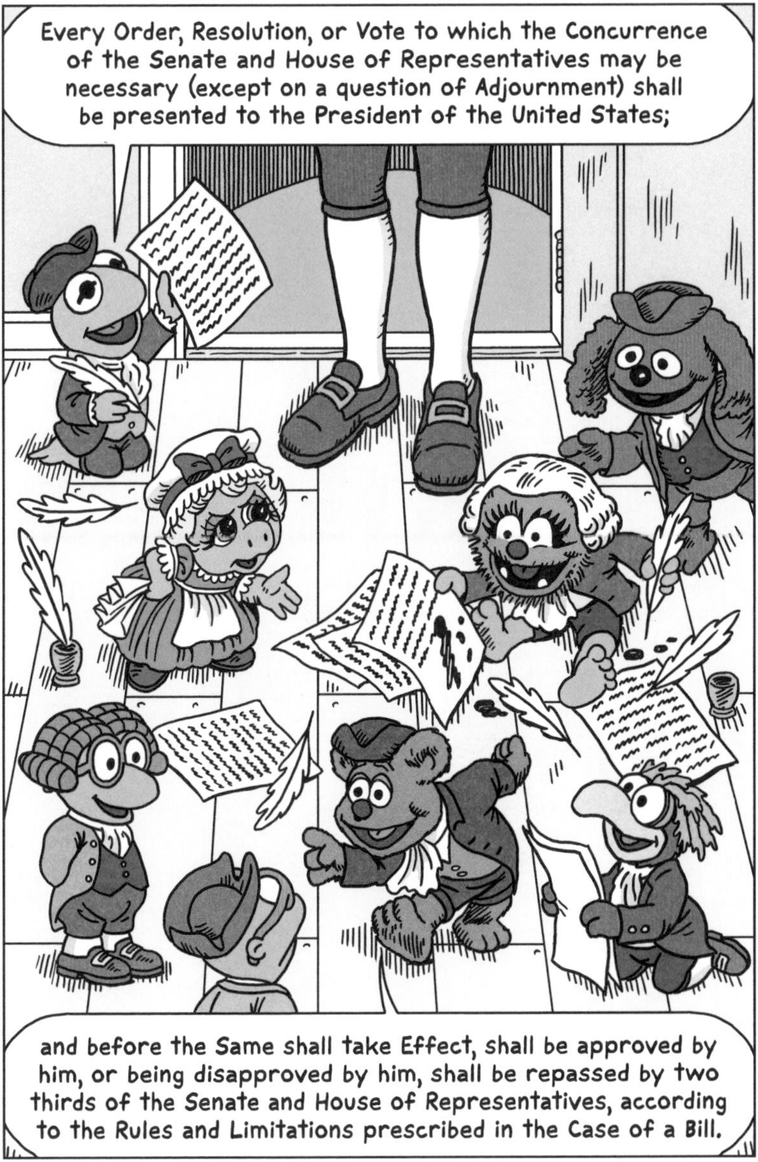
Every Order, Resolution, or Vote to which the Concurrence of the Senate and House of Representatives may be necessary (except on a question of Adjournment) shall be presented to the President of the United States;
and before the Same shall take Effect, shall be approved by him, or being disapproved by him, shall be repassed by two thirds of the Senate and House of Representatives, according to the Rules and Limitations prescribed in the Case of a Bill.

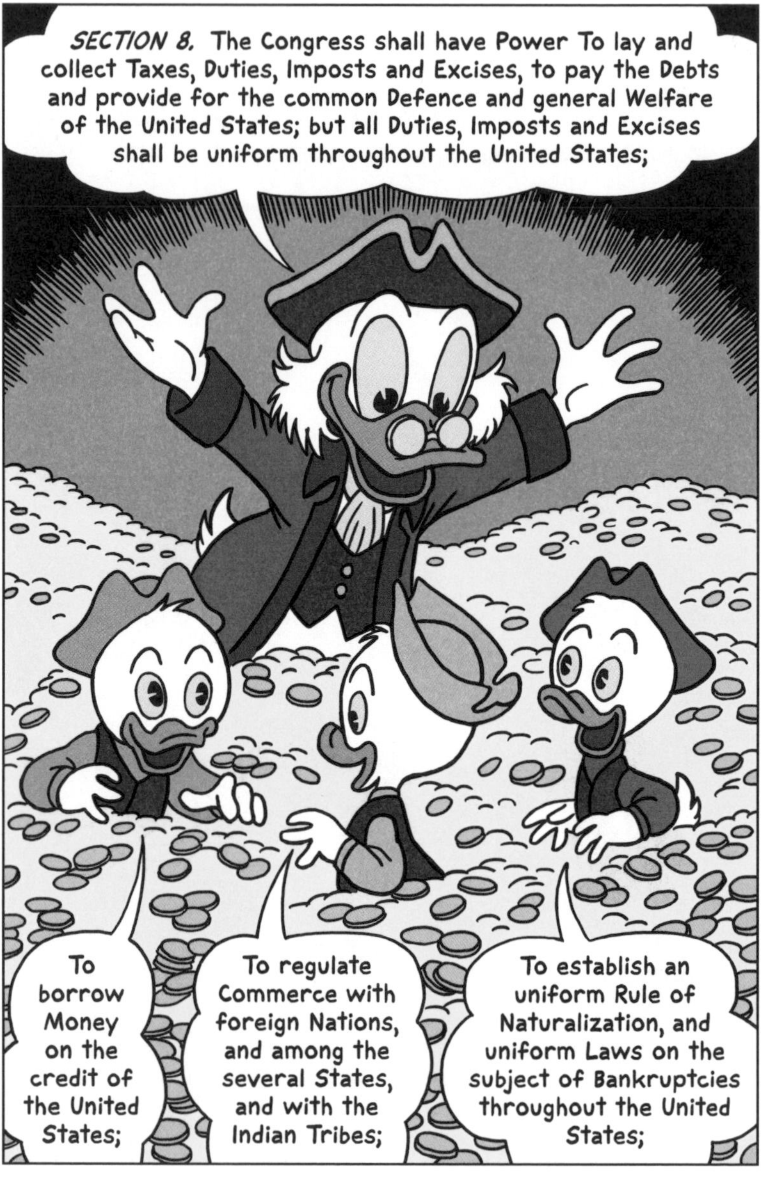
SECTION 8. The Congress shall have Power To lay and collect Taxes, Duties, Imposts and Excises, to pay the Debts and provide for the common Defence and general Welfare of the United States; but all Duties, Imposts and Excises shall be uniform throughout the United States;
To borrow Money on the credit of the United States;
To regulate Commerce with foreign Nations, and among the several States, and with the Indian Tribes;
To establish an uniform Rule of Naturalization, and uniform Laws on the subject of Bankruptcies throughout the United States;

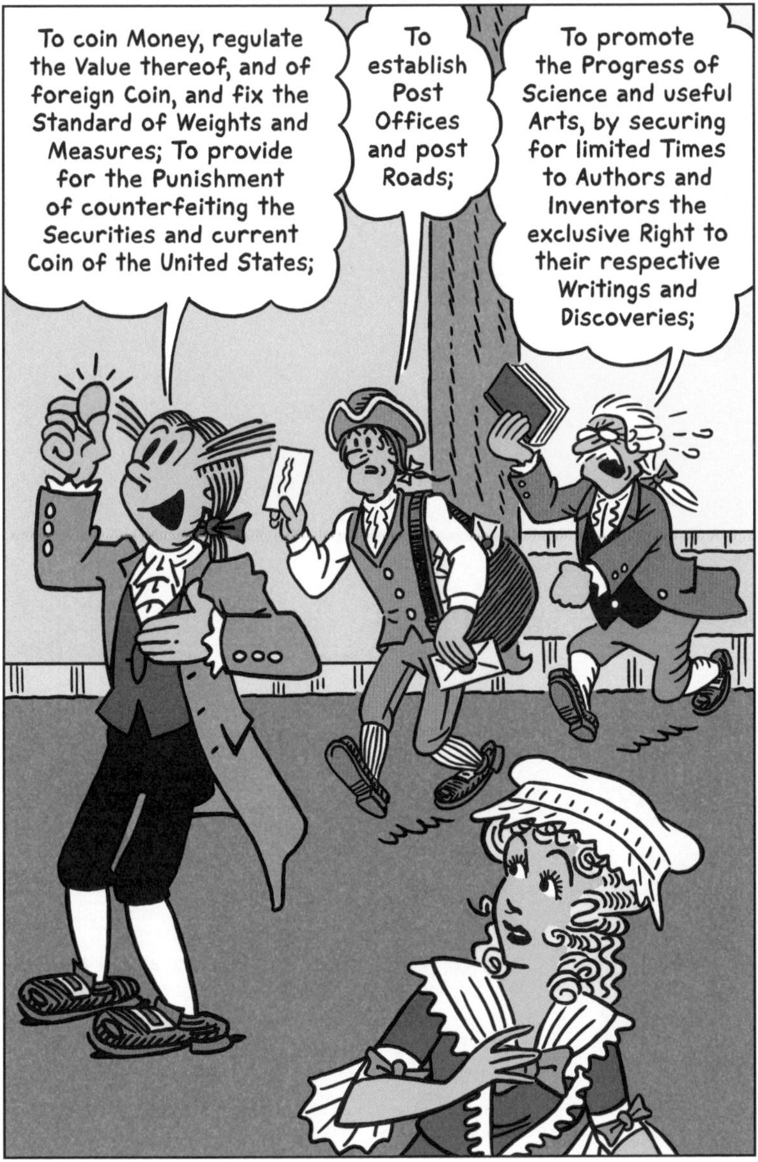
To coin Money, regulate the Value thereof, and of foreign Coin, and fix the Standard of Weights and Measures; To provide for the Punishment of counterfeiting the Securities and current Coin of the United States;
To establish Post Offices and post Roads;
To promote the Progress of Science and useful Arts, by securing for limited Times to Authors and Inventors the exclusive Right to their respective Writings and Discoveries;

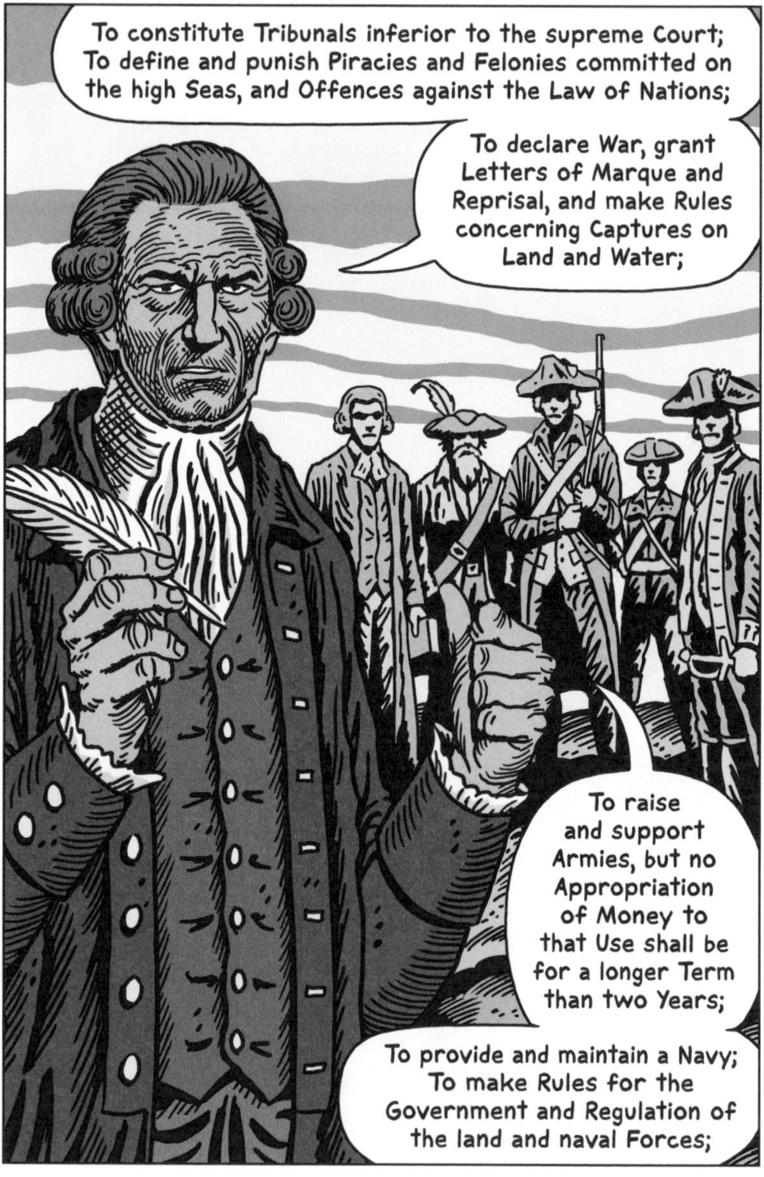
To constitute Tribunals inferior to the supreme Court; To define and punish Piracies and Felonies committed on the high Seas, and Offences against the Law of Nations;
To declare War, grant Letters of Marque and Reprisal, and make Rules concerning Captures on Land and Water;
To raise and support Armies, but no Appropriation of Money to that Use shall be for a longer Term than two Years;
To provide and maintain a Navy; To make Rules for the Government and Regulation of the land and naval Forces;

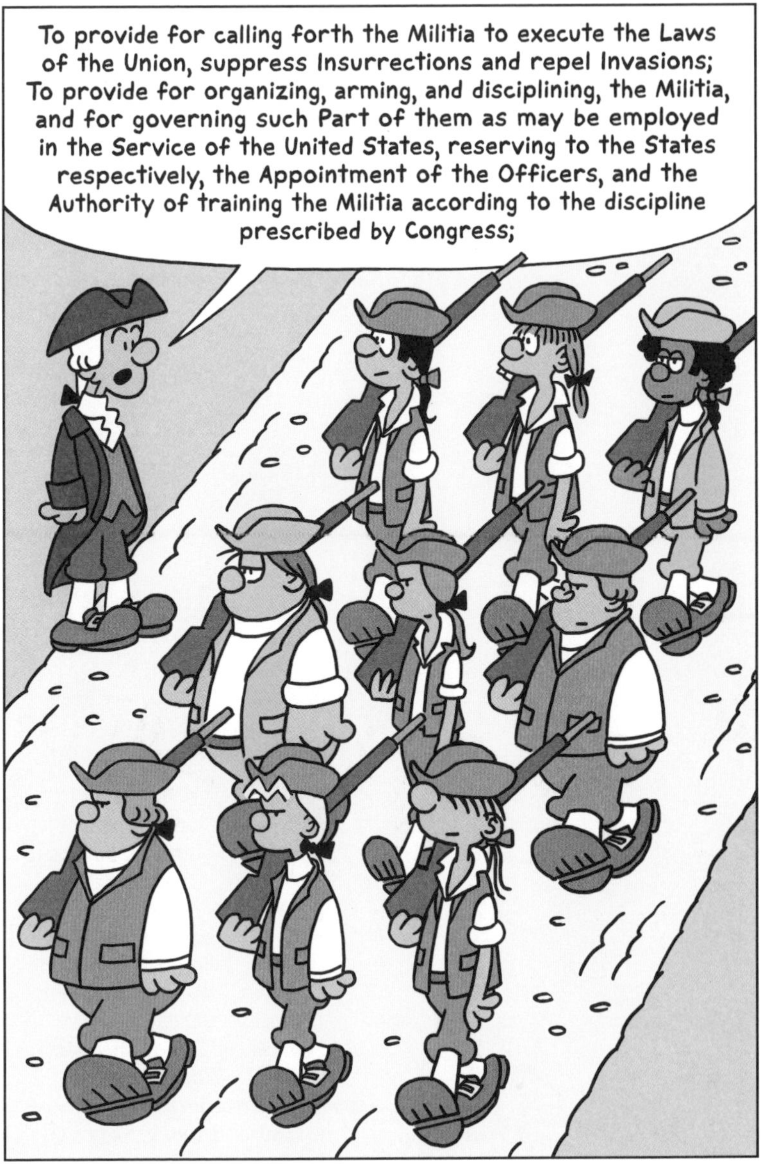
To provide for calling forth the Militia to execute the Laws of the Union, suppress Insurrections and repel Invasions; To provide for organizing, arming, and disciplining, the Militia, and for governing such Part of them as may be employed in the Service of the United States, reserving to the States respectively, the Appointment of the Officers, and the Authority of training the Militia according to the discipline prescribed by Congress;

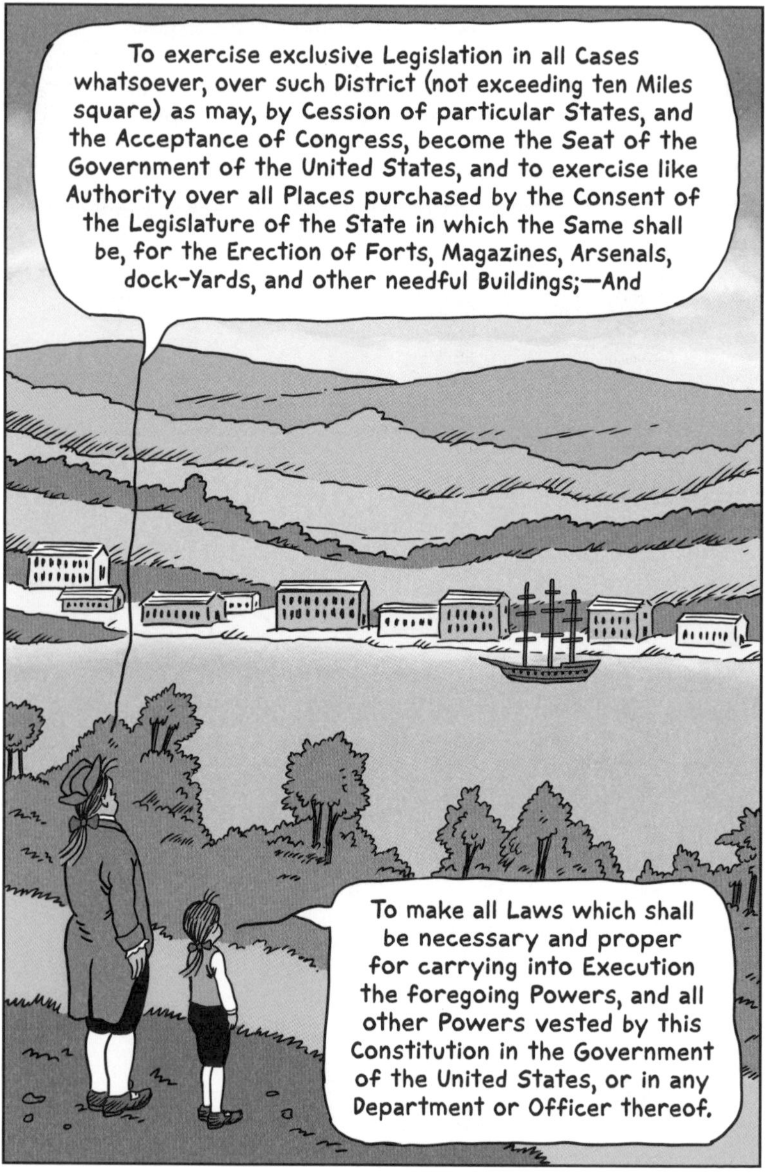
To exercise exclusive Legislation in all Cases whatsoever, over such District (not exceeding ten Miles square) as may, by Cession of particular States, and the Acceptance of Congress, become the Seat of the Government of the United States, and to exercise like Authority over all Places purchased by the Consent of the Legislature of the State in which the Same shall be, for the Erection of Forts, Magazines, Arsenals, dock-Yards, and other needful Buildings;—And
To make all Laws which shall be necessary and proper for carrying into Execution the foregoing Powers, and all other Powers vested by this Constitution in the Government of the United States, or in any Department or Officer thereof.

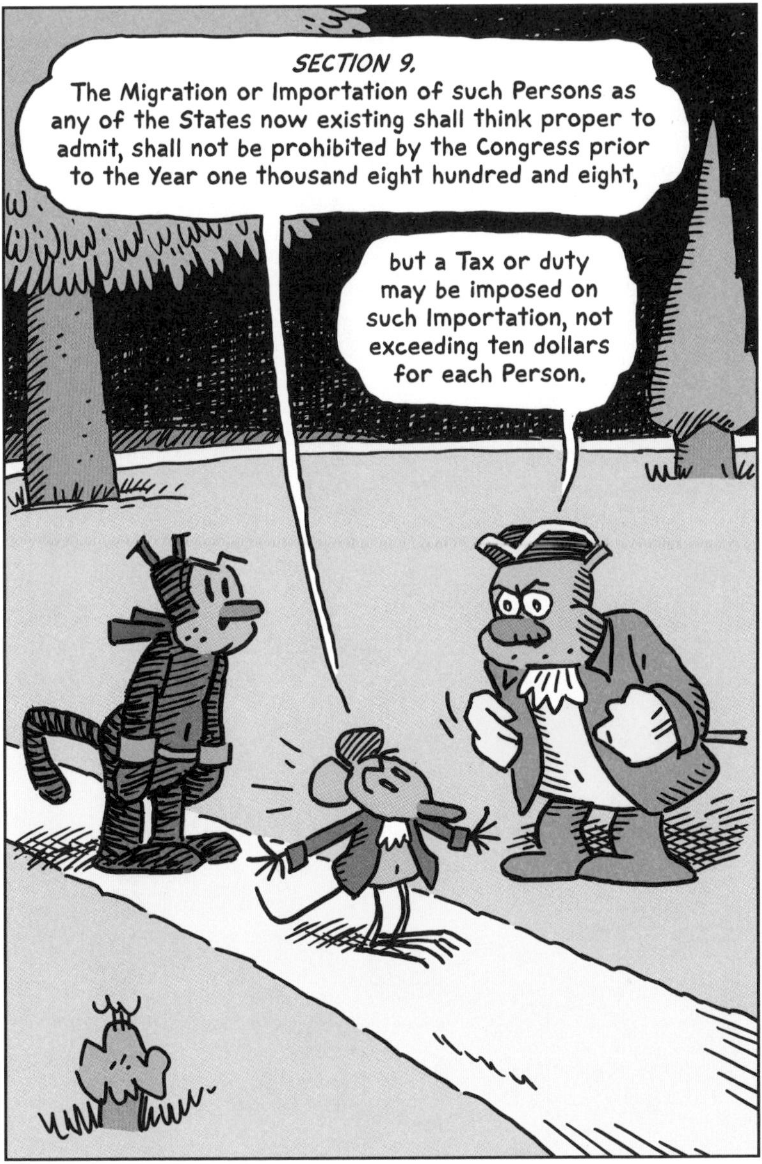
SECTION 9.
The Migration or Importation of such Persons as any of the States now existing shall think proper to admit, shall not be prohibited by the Congress prior to the Year one thousand eight hundred and eight,
but a Tax or duty may be imposed on such Importation, not exceeding ten dollars for each Person.

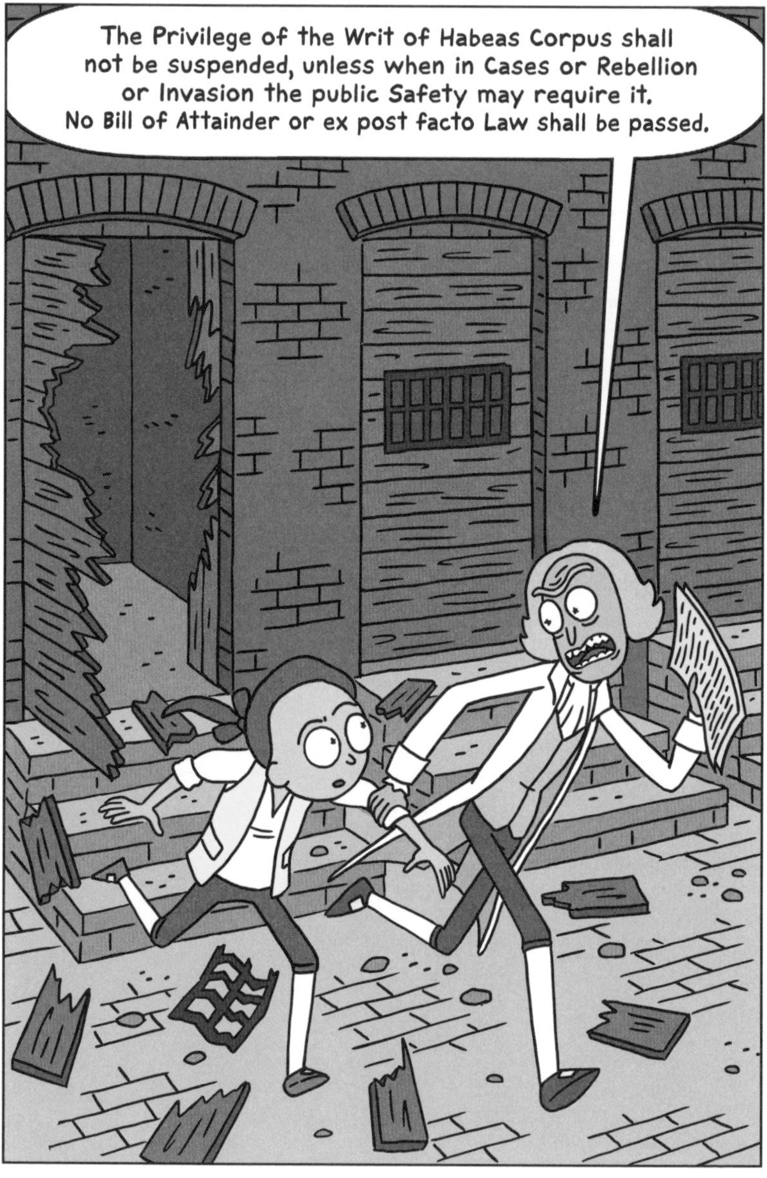
The Privilege of the Writ of Habeas Corpus shall not be suspended, unless when in Cases or Rebellion or Invasion the public Safety may require it. No Bill of Attainder or ex post facto Law shall be passed.

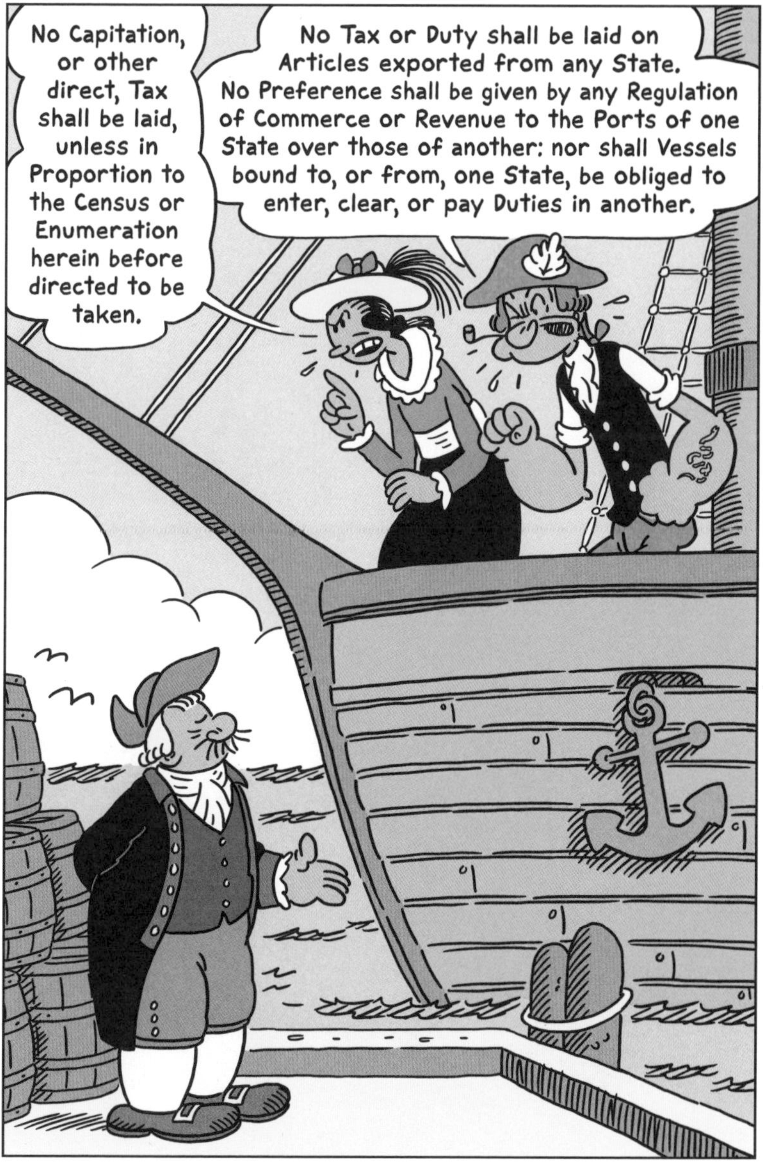
No Capitation, or other direct, Tax shall be laid, unless in Proportion to the Census or Enumeration herein before directed to be taken.
No Tax or Duty shall be laid on Articles exported from any State. No Preference shall be given by any Regulation of Commerce or Revenue to the Ports of one State over those of another: nor shall Vessels bound to, or from, one State, be obliged to enter, clear, or pay Duties in another.

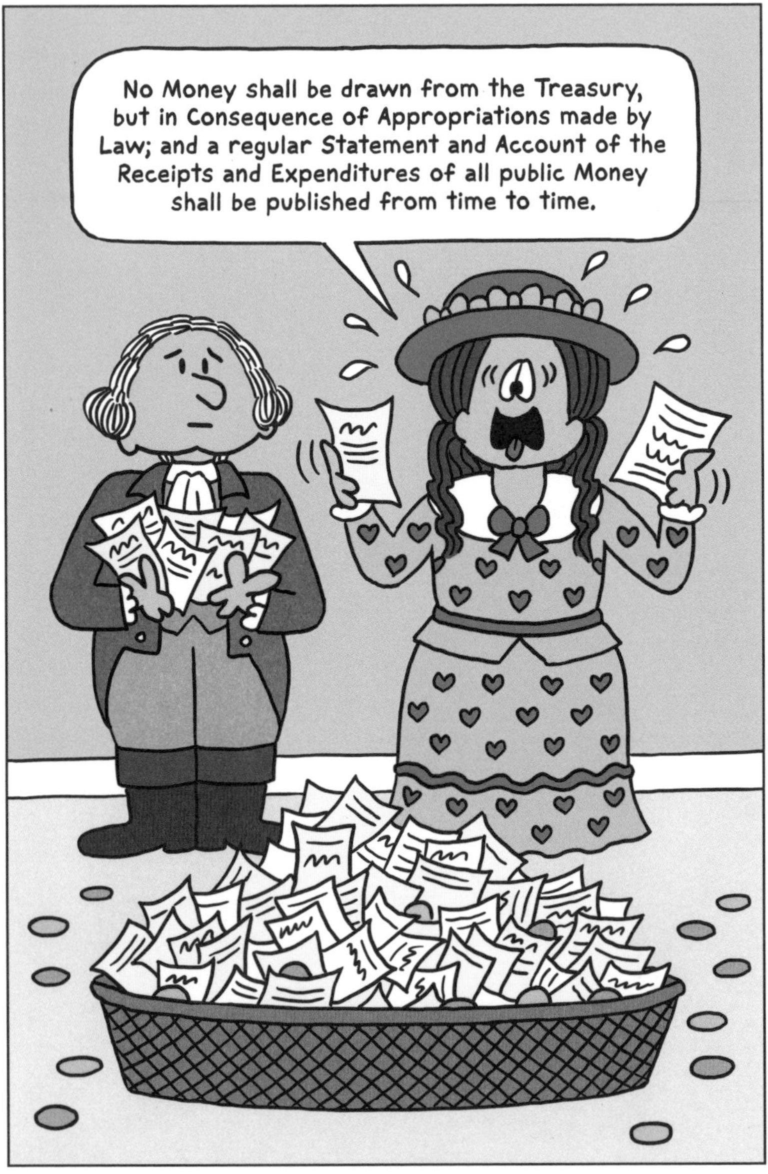
No Money shall be drawn from the Treasury, but in Consequence of Appropriations made by Law; and a regular Statement and Account of the Receipts and Expenditures of all public Money shall be published from time to time.

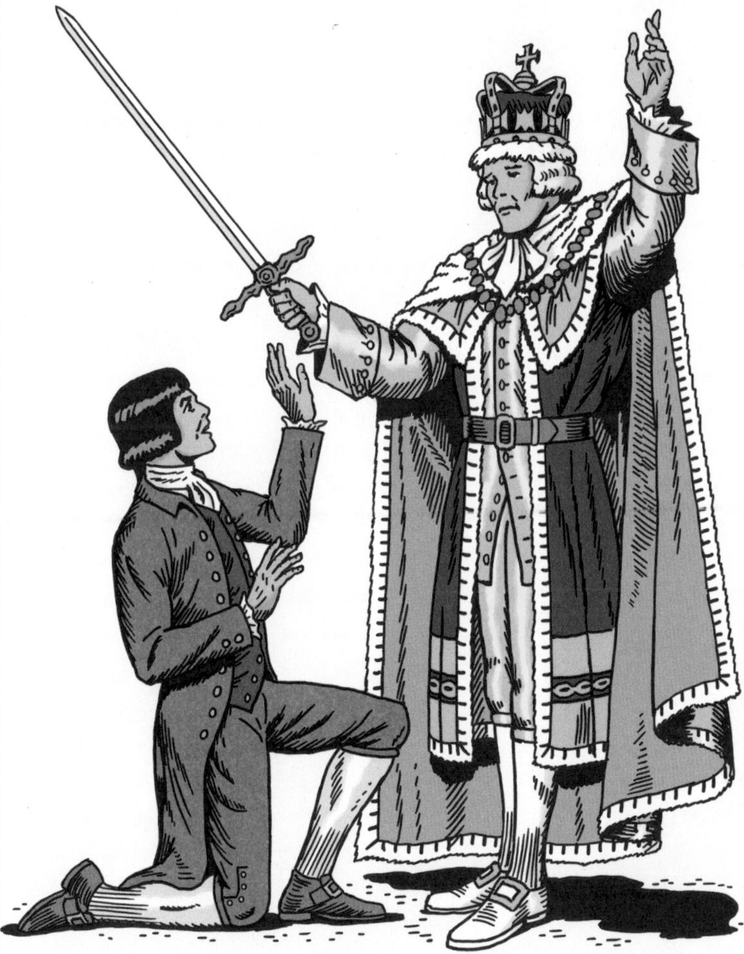

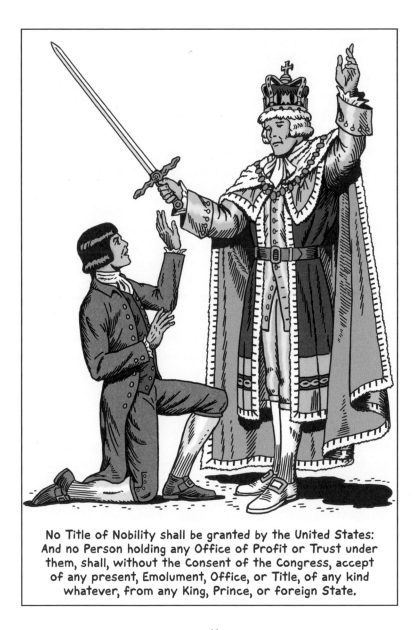

No Title of Nobility shall be granted by the United States: And no Person holding any Office of Profit or Trust under them, shall, without the Consent of the Congress, accept of any present, Emolument, Office, or Title, of any kind whatever, from any King, Prince, or foreign State.

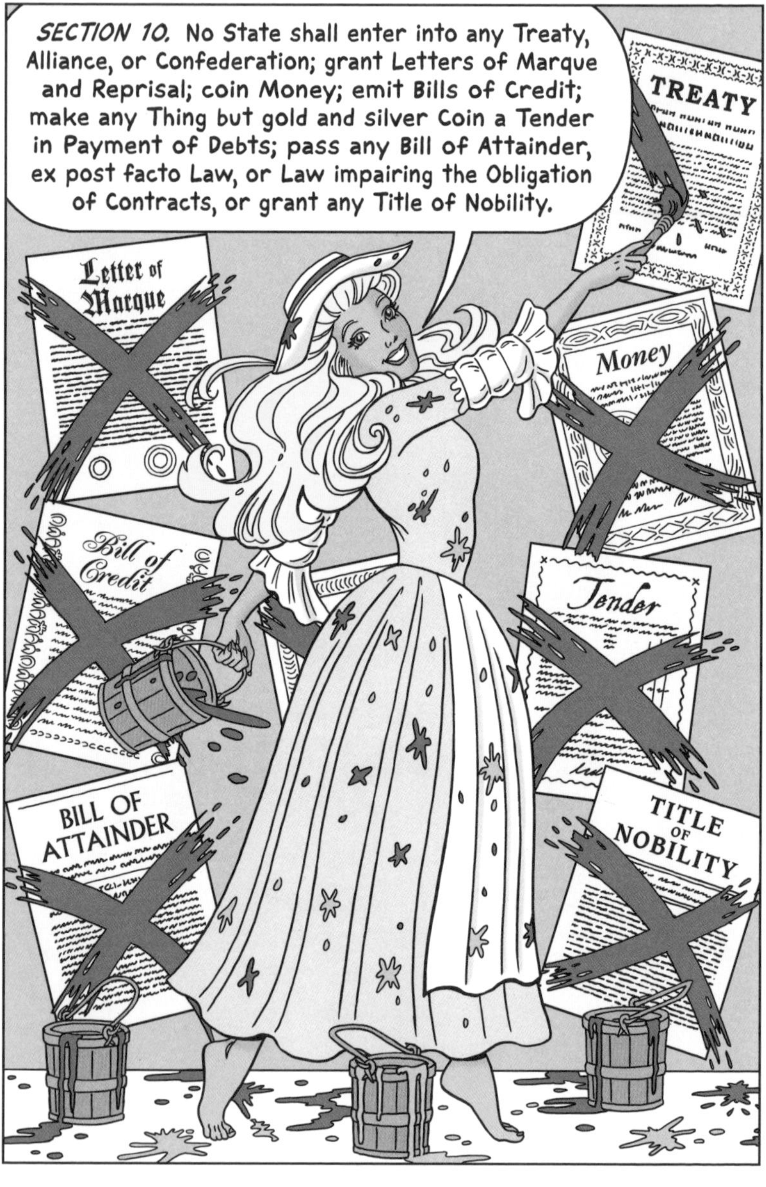
SECTION 10. No State shall enter into any Treaty, Alliance, or Confederation; grant Letters of Marque and Reprisal; coin Money; emit Bills of Credit; make any Thing but gold and silver Coin a Tender in Payment of Debts; pass any Bill of Attainder, ex post facto Law, or Law impairing the Obligation of Contracts, or grant any Title of Nobility.
TREATY
Letter of Marque
Money
Bill of Credit
Tender
BILL OF ATTAINDER
TITLE OF NOBILITY

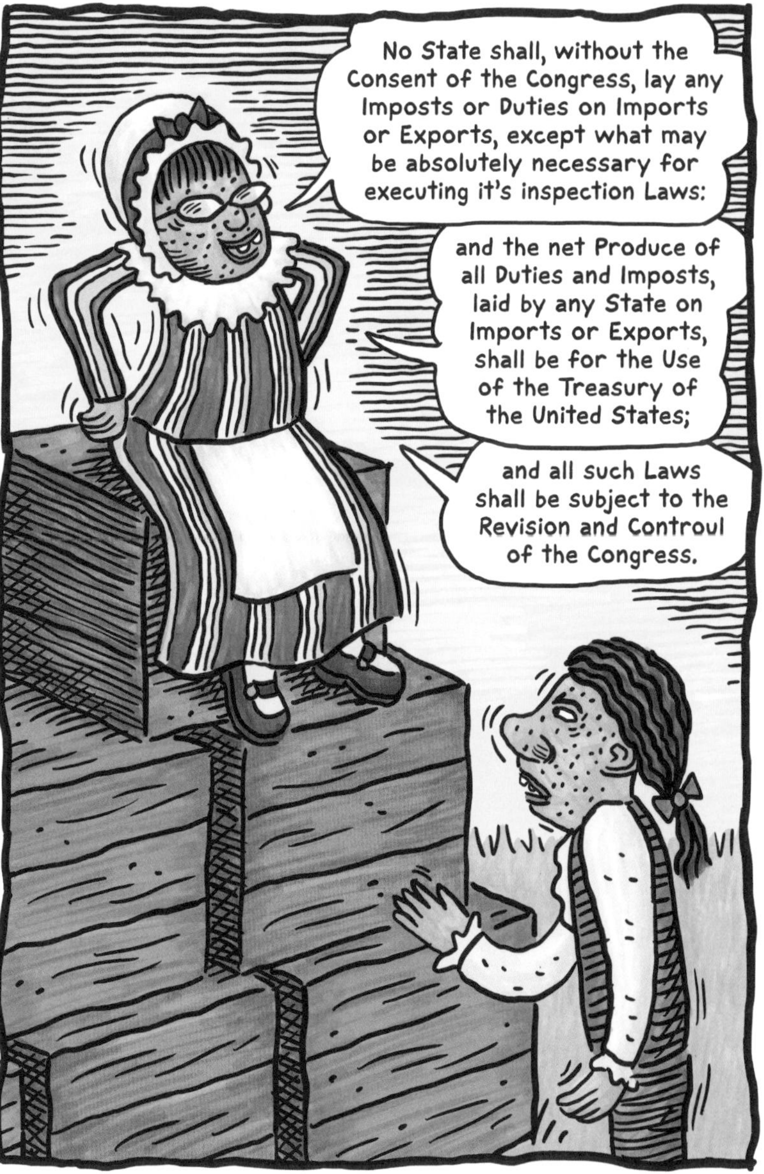
No State shall, without the Consent of the Congress, lay any Imposts or Duties on Imports or Exports, except what may be absolutely necessary for executing it's inspection Laws:
and the net Produce of all Duties and Imposts, laid by any State on Imports or Exports, shall be for the Use of the Treasury of the United States;
and all such Laws shall be subject to the Revision and Controul of the Congress.

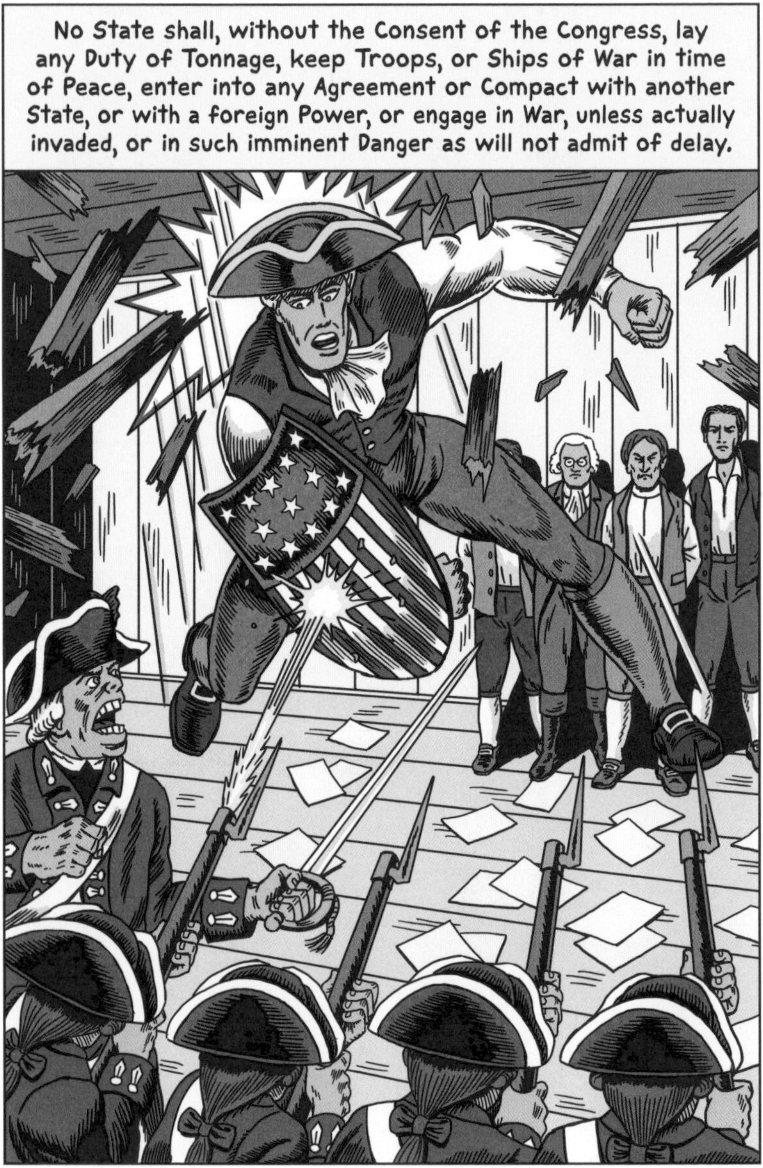
No State shall, without the Consent of the Congress, lay any Duty of Tonnage, keep Troops, or Ships of War in time of Peace, enter into any Agreement or Compact with another State, or with a foreign Power, or engage in War, unless actually invaded, or in such imminent Danger as will not admit of delay.

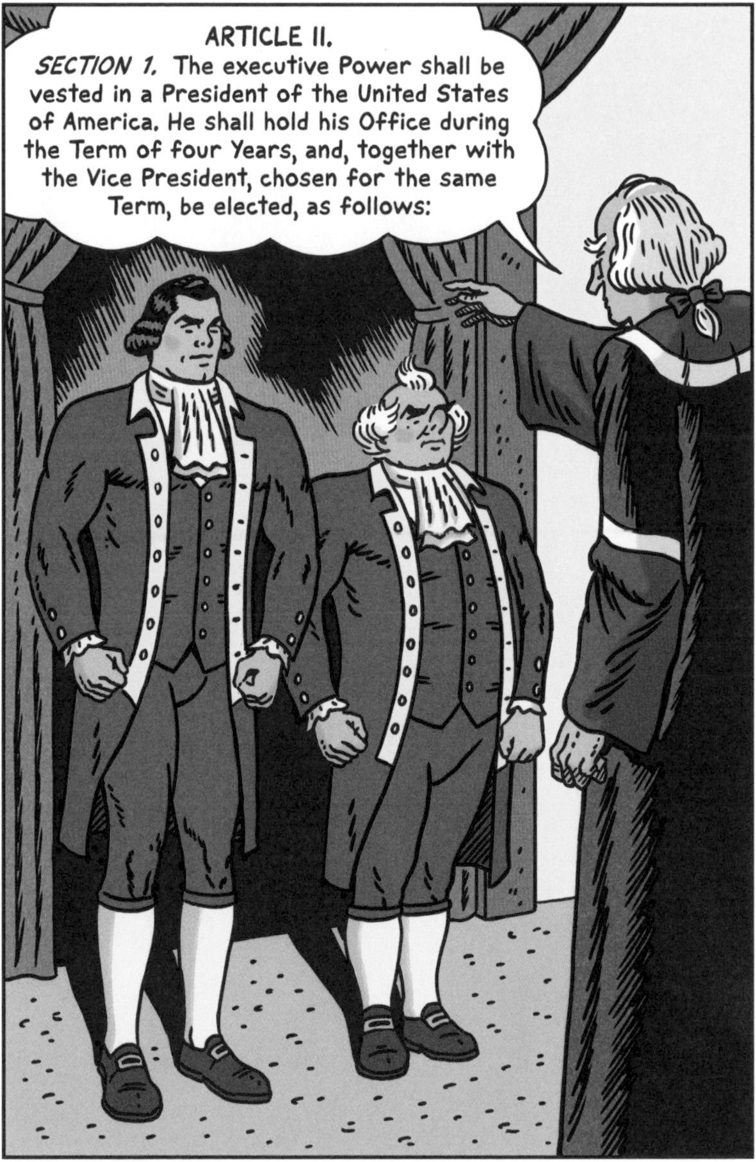
ARTICLE II.
SECTION 1. The executive Power shall be vested in a President of the United States of America. He shall hold his Office during the Term of four Years, and, together with the Vice President, chosen for the same Term, be elected, as follows:

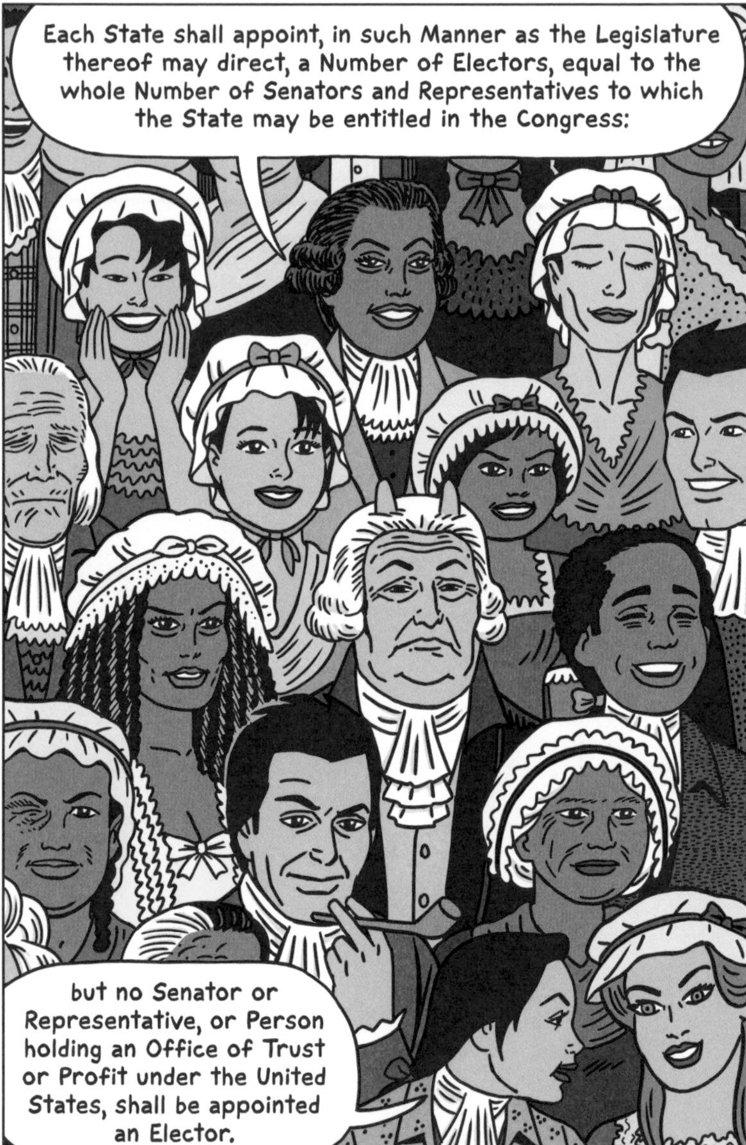
Each State shall appoint, in such Manner as the Legislature thereof may direct, a Number of Electors, equal to the whole Number of Senators and Representatives to which the State may be entitled in the Congress:
but no Senator or Representative, or Person holding an Office of Trust or Profit under the United States, shall be appointed an Elector.

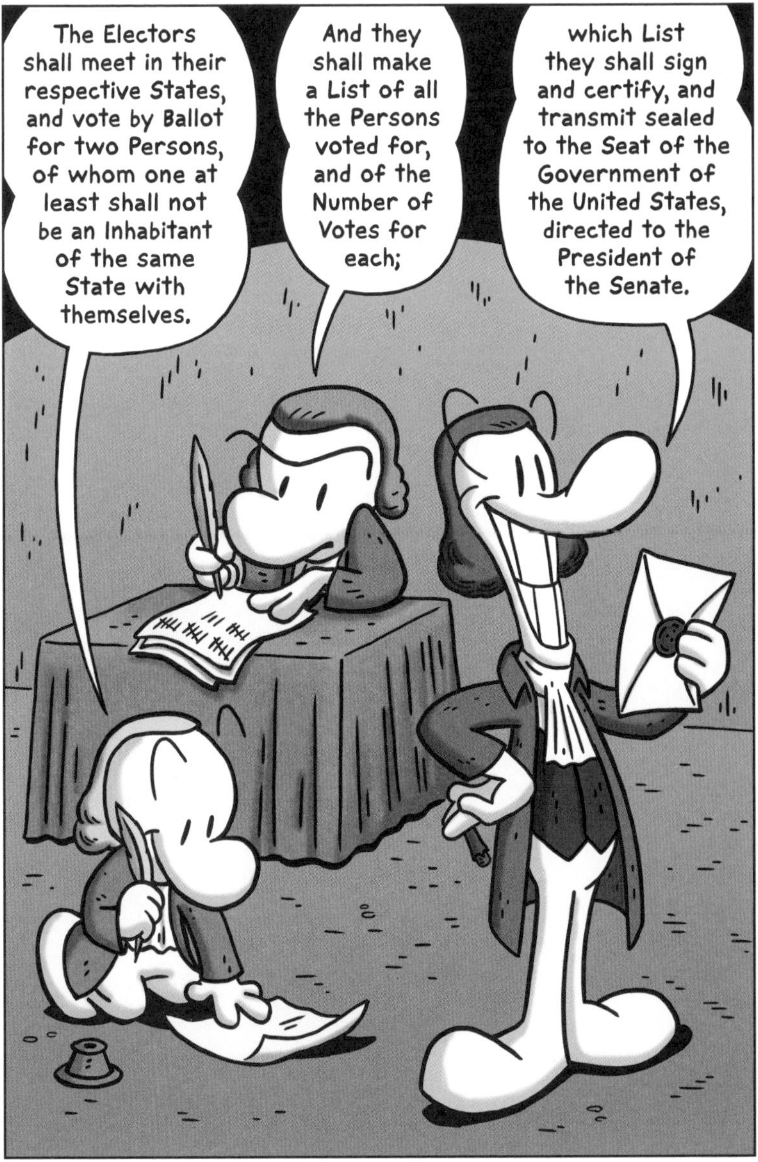
The Electors shall meet in their respective States, and vote by Ballot for two Persons, of whom one at least shall not be an Inhabitant of the same State with themselves.
And they shall make a List of all the Persons voted for, and of the Number of Votes for each;
which List they shall sign and certify, and transmit sealed to the Seat of the Government of the United States, directed to the President of the Senate.

In every Case, after the Choice of the President, the Person having the greatest Number of Votes of the Electors shall be the Vice President. But if there should remain two or more who have equal Votes, the Senate shall chuse from them by Ballot the Vice President.

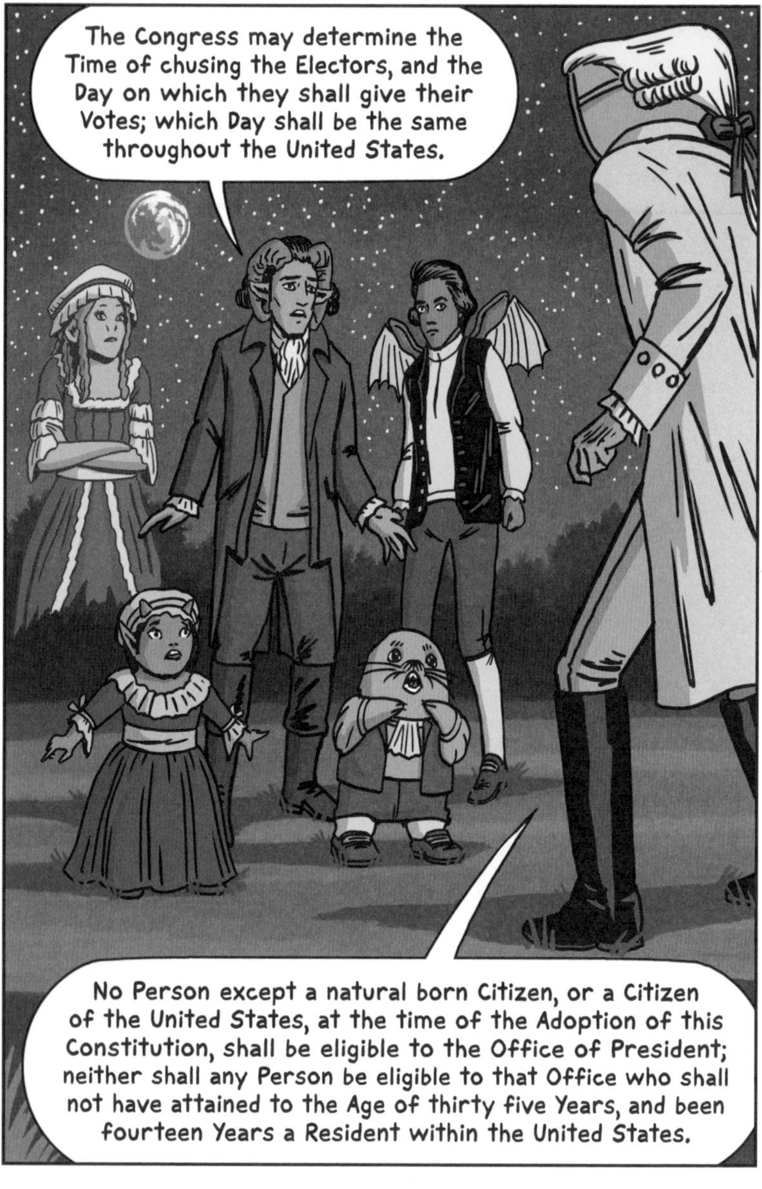
The Congress may determine the Time of chusing the Electors, and the Day on which they shall give their Votes; which Day shall be the same throughout the United States.
No Person except a natural born Citizen, or a Citizen of the United States, at the time of the Adoption of this Constitution, shall be eligible to the Office of President; neither shall any Person be eligible to that Office who shall not have attained to the Age of thirty five Years, and been fourteen Years a Resident within the United States.

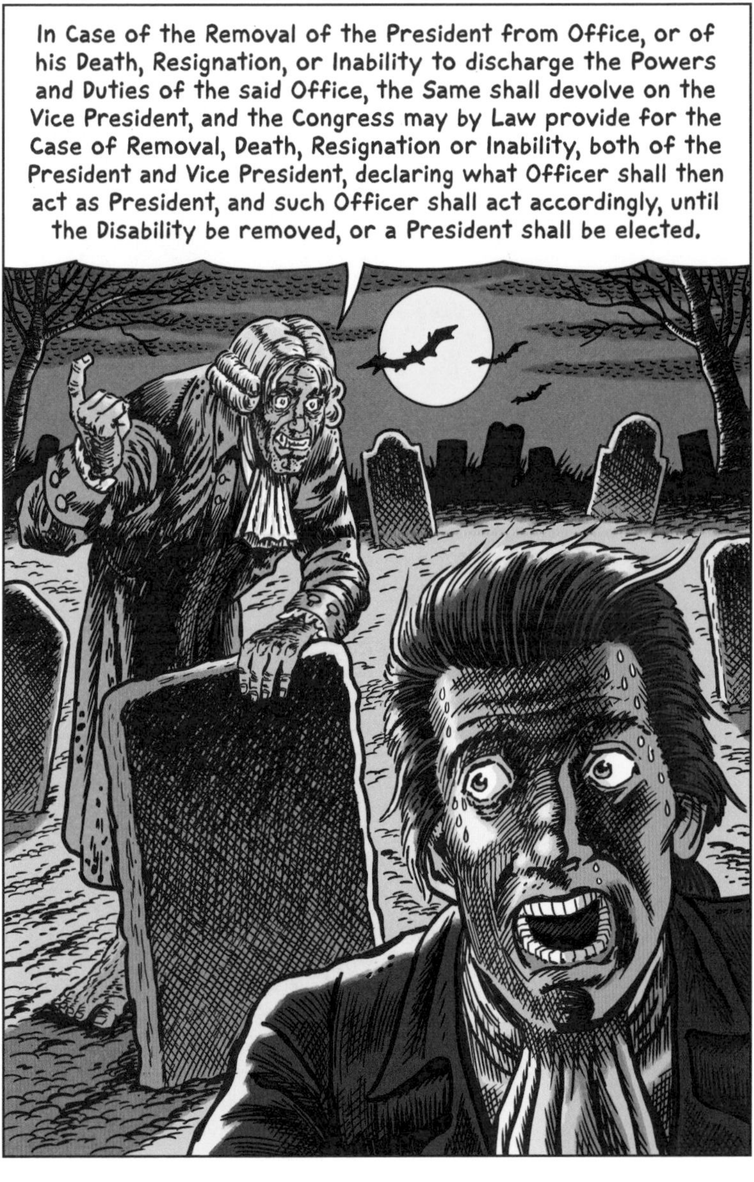
In Case of the Removal of the President from Office, or of his Death, Resignation, or Inability to discharge the Powers and Duties of the said Office, the Same shall devolve on the Vice President, and the Congress may by Law provide for the Case of Removal, Death, Resignation or Inability, both of the President and Vice President, declaring what Officer shall then act as President, and such Officer shall act accordingly, until the Disability be removed, or a President shall be elected.

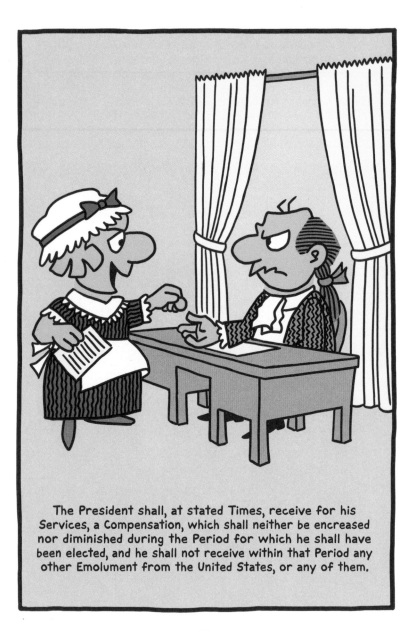

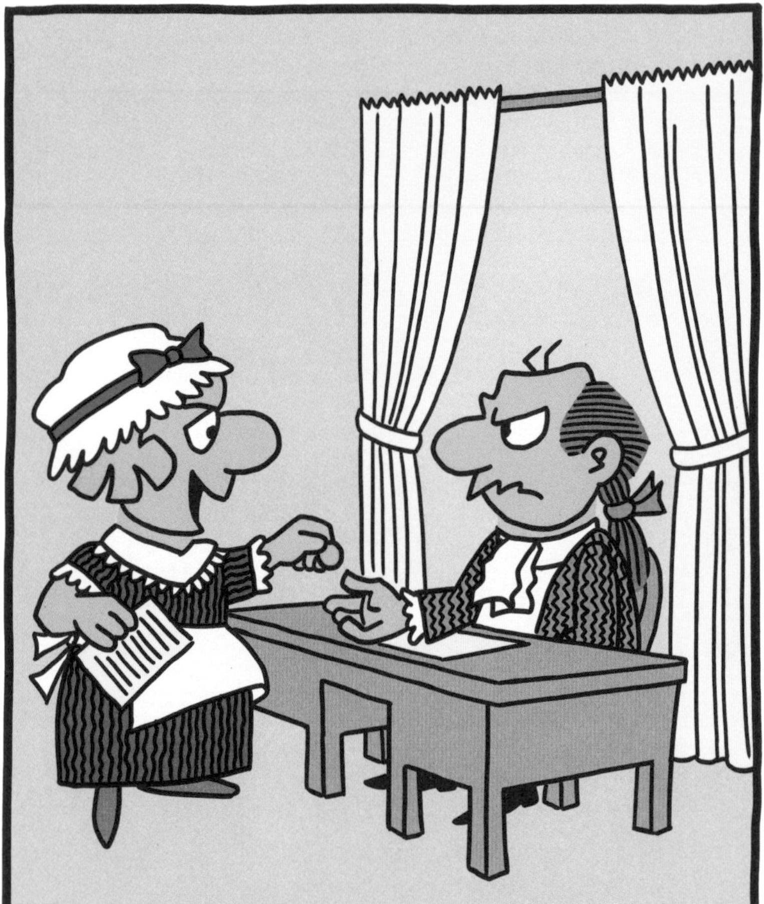
The President shall, at stated Times, receive for his Services, a Compensation, which shall neither be encreased nor diminished during the Period for which he shall have been elected, and he shall not receive within that Period any other Emolument from the United States, or any of them.

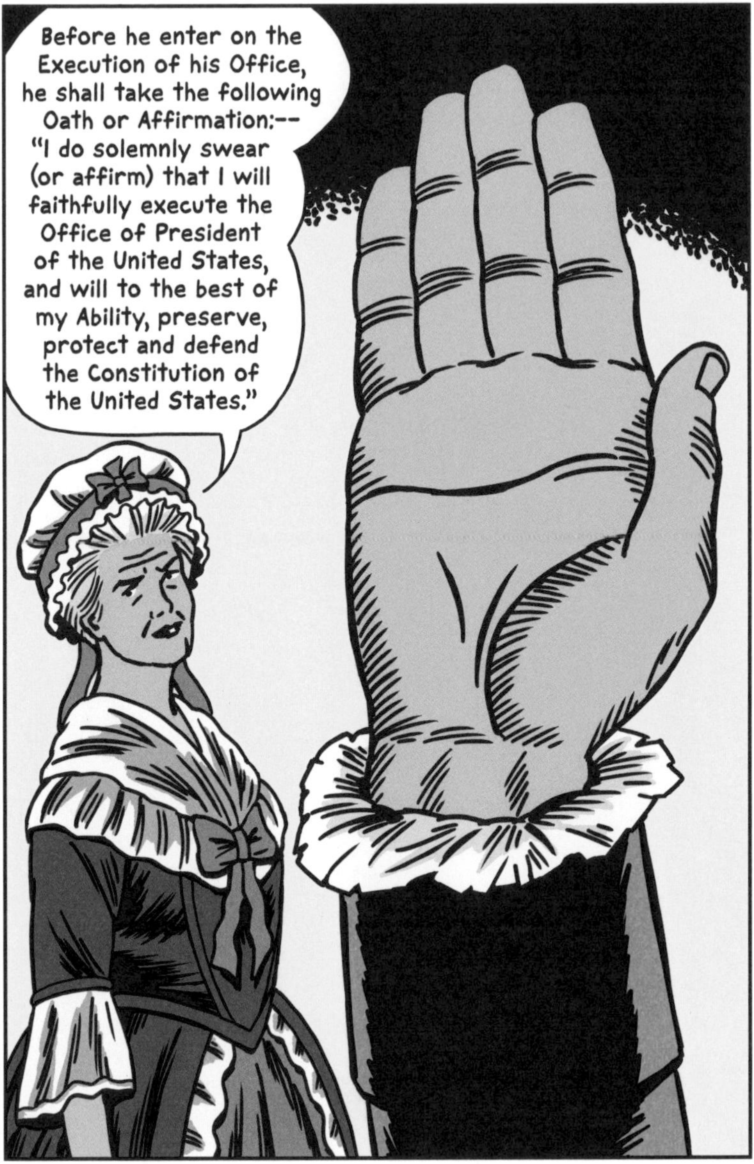
Before he enter on the Execution of his Office, he shall take the following Oath or Affirmation:-- "I do solemnly swear (or affirm) that I will faithfully execute the Office of President of the United States, and will to the best of my Ability, preserve, protect and defend the Constitution of the United States."

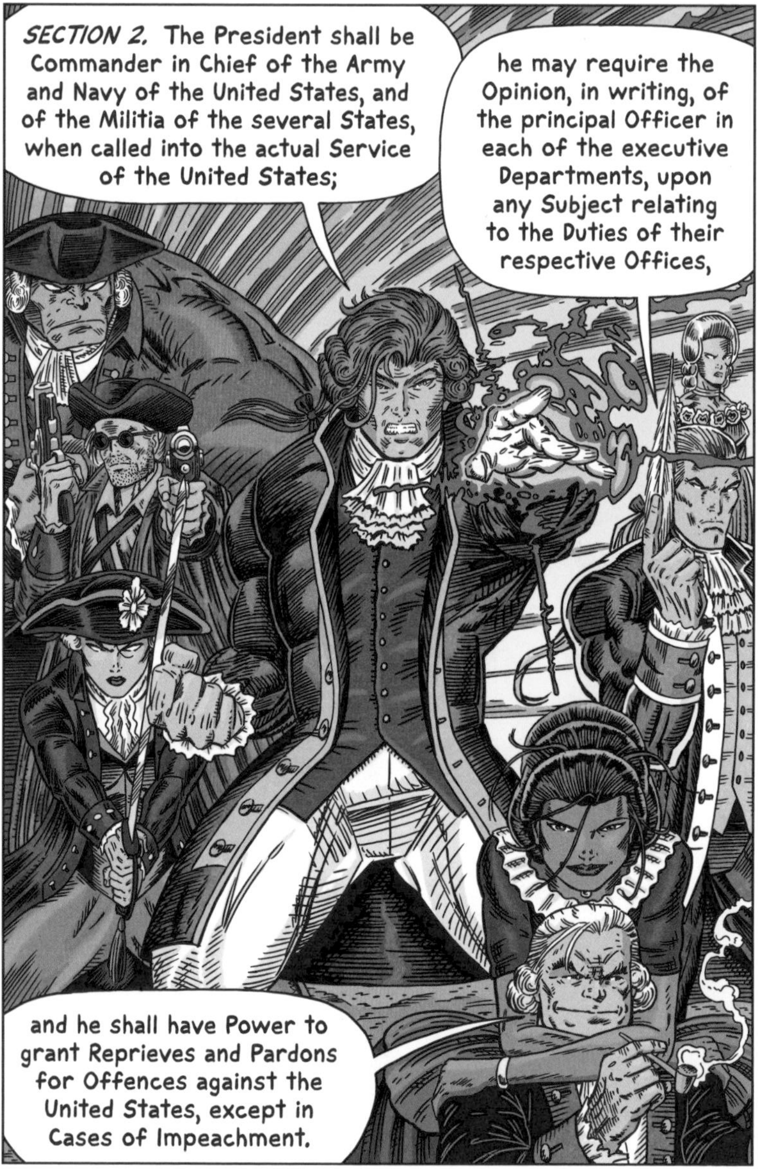
SECTION 2. The President shall be Commander in Chief of the Army and Navy of the United States, and of the Militia of the several States, when called into the actual Service of the United States;
he may require the Opinion, in writing, of the principal Officer in each of the executive Departments, upon any Subject relating to the Duties of their respective Offices,
and he shall have Power to grant Reprieves and Pardons for Offences against the United States, except in Cases of Impeachment.

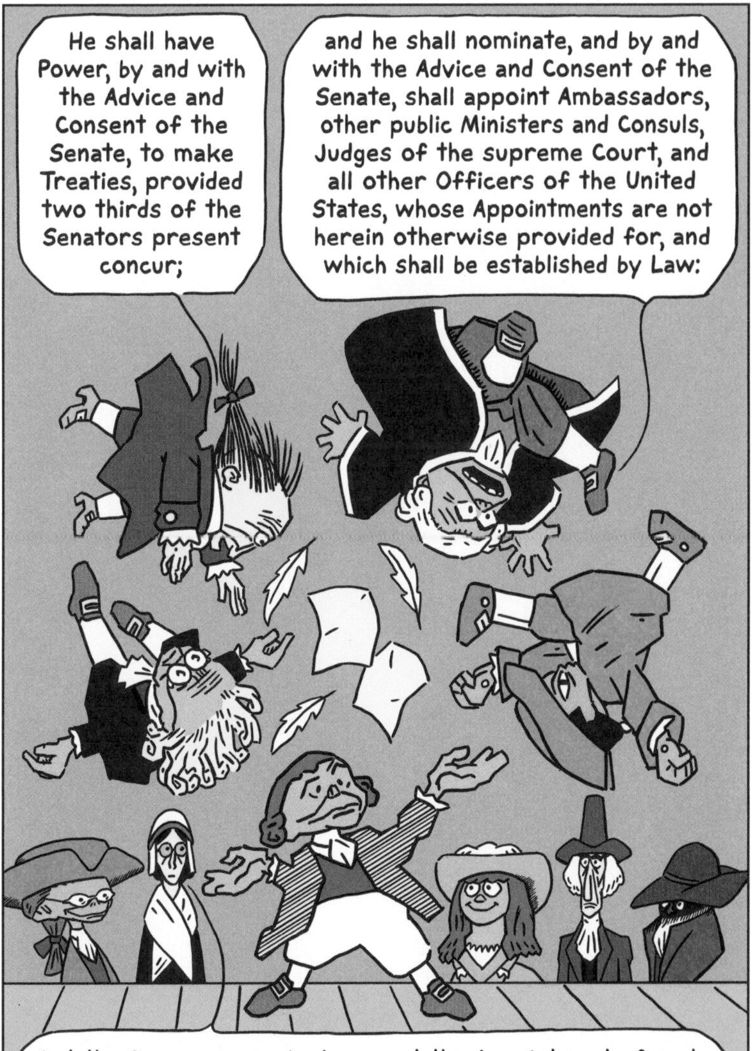
He shall have Power, by and with the Advice and Consent of the Senate, to make Treaties, provided two thirds of the Senators present concur;
and he shall nominate, and by and with the Advice and Consent of the Senate, shall appoint Ambassadors, other public Ministers and Consuls, Judges of the supreme Court, and all other Officers of the United States, whose Appointments are not herein otherwise provided for, and which shall be established by Law:
but the Congress may by Law vest the Appointment of such inferior Officers, as they think proper, in the President alone, in the Courts of Law, or in the Heads of Departments.

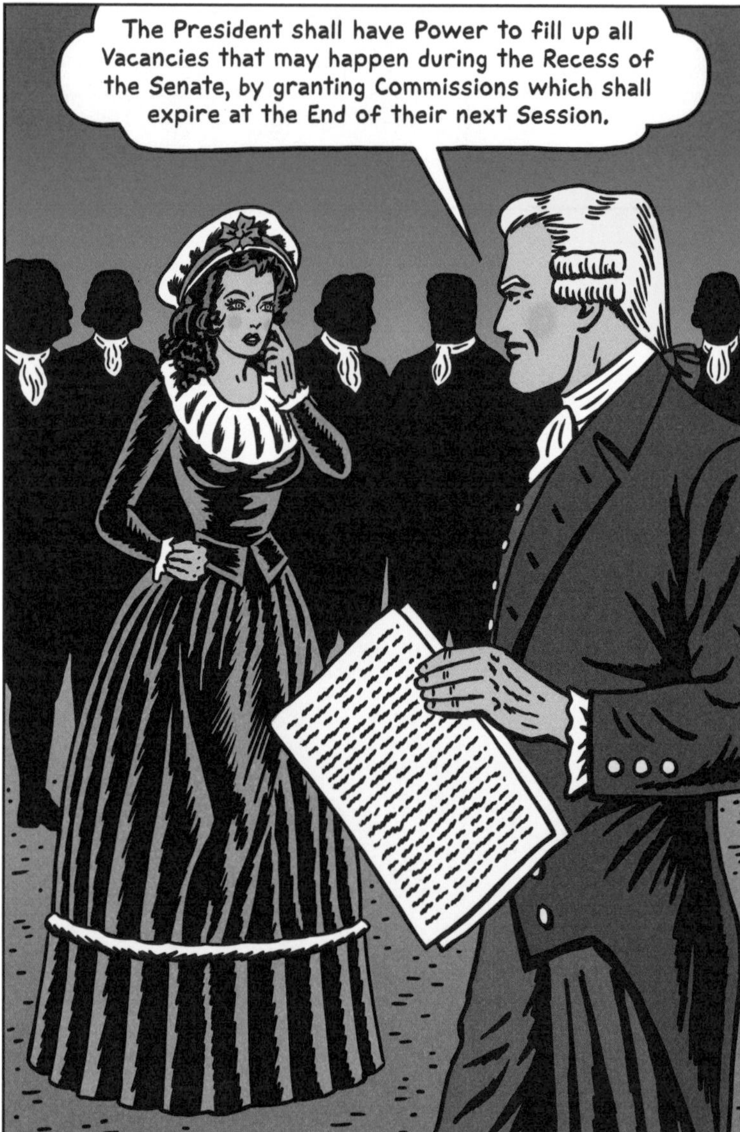
The President shall have Power to fill up all Vacancies that may happen during the Recess of the Senate, by granting Commissions which shall expire at the End of their next Session.

SECTION 3. He shall from time to time give to the Congress Information on the State of the Union, and recommend to their Consideration such Measures as he shall judge necessary and expedient; he may, on extraordinary Occasions, convene both Houses, or either of them, and in Case of Disagreement between them, with Respect to the Time of Adjournment, he may adjourn them to such Time as he shall think proper;

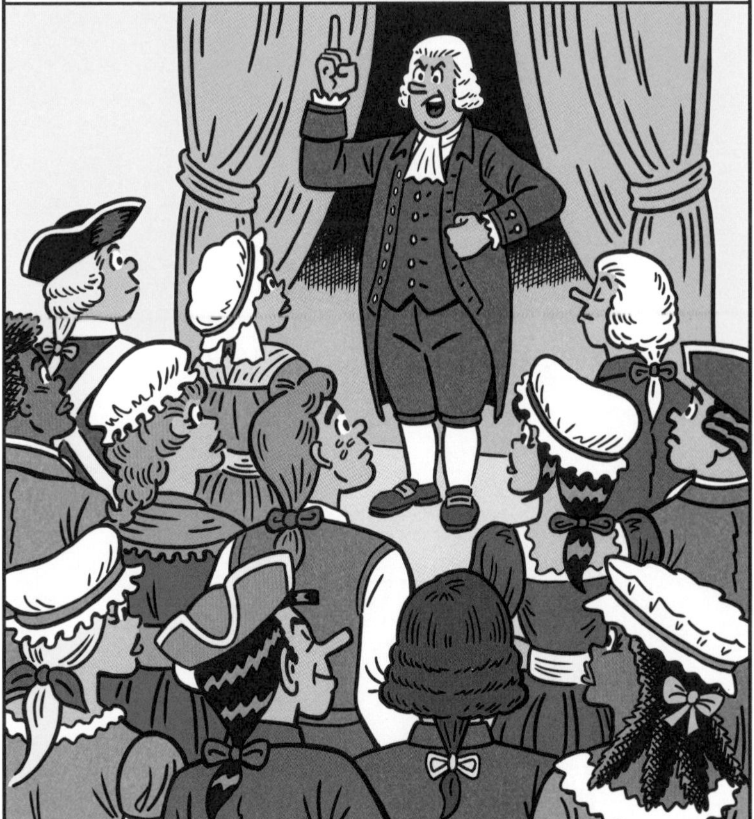

he shall receive Ambassadors and other public Ministers; he shall take Care that the Laws be faithfully executed, and shall Commission all the Officers of the United States.

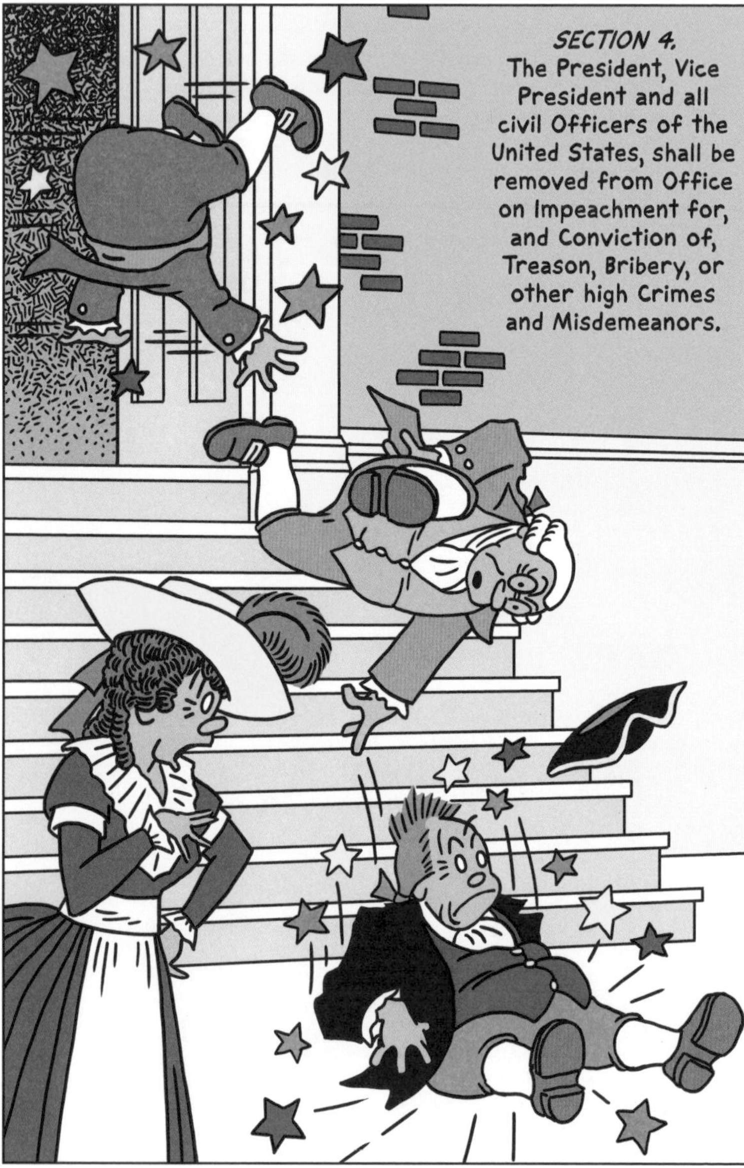
SECTION 4.
The President, Vice President and all civil Officers of the United States, shall be removed from Office on Impeachment for, and Conviction of, Treason, Bribery, or other high Crimes and Misdemeanors.

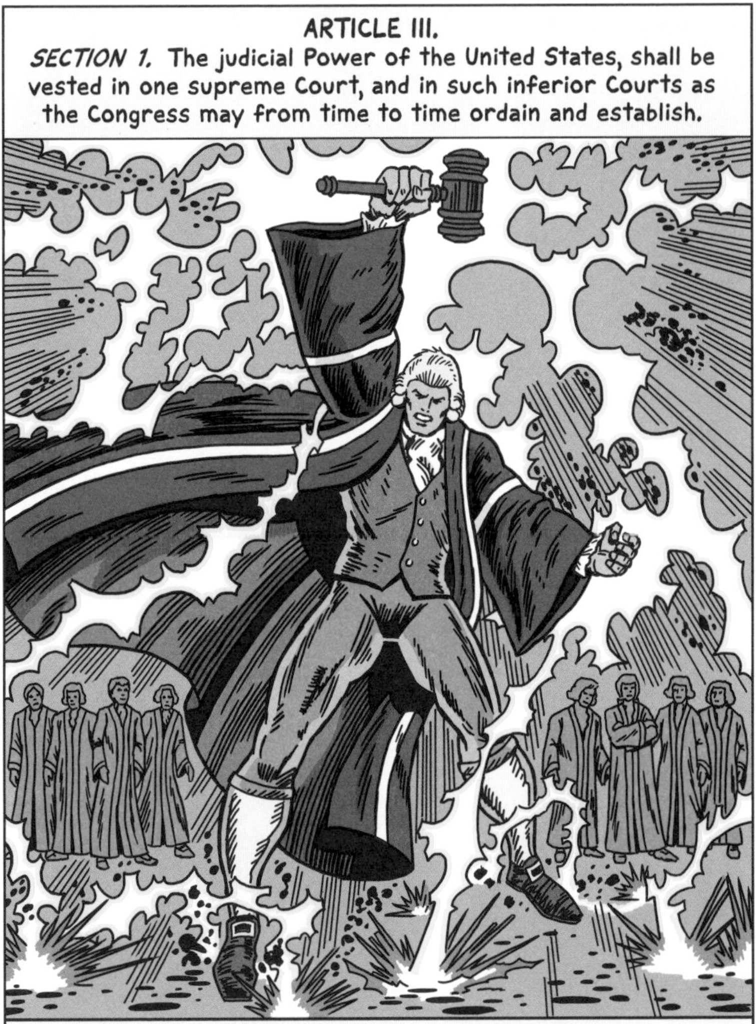
ARTICLE III.
SECTION 1. The judicial Power of the United States, shall be vested in one supreme Court, and in such inferior Courts as the Congress may from time to time ordain and establish.
The Judges, both of the supreme and inferior Courts, shall hold their Offices during good Behaviour, and shall, at stated Times, receive for their Services, a Compensation, which shall not be diminished during their Continuance in Office.

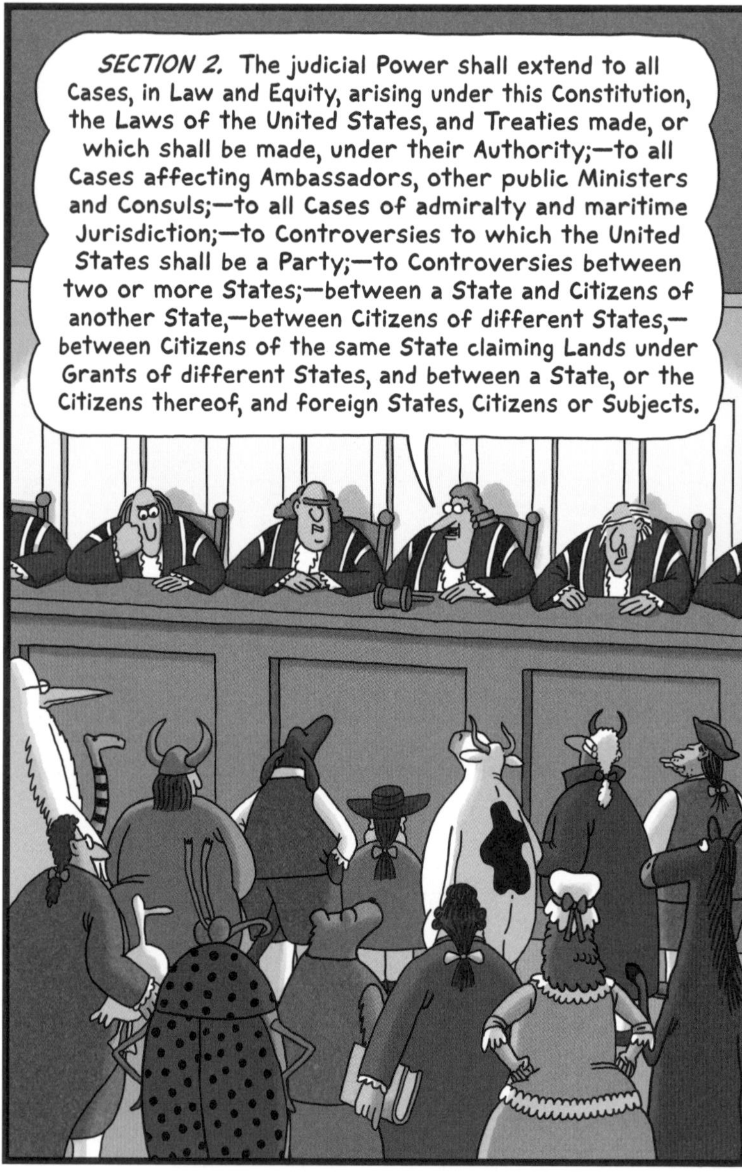
SECTION 2. The judicial Power shall extend to all Cases, in Law and Equity, arising under this Constitution, the Laws of the United States, and Treaties made, or which shall be made, under their Authority;—to all Cases affecting Ambassadors, other public Ministers and Consuls;—to all Cases of admiralty and maritime Jurisdiction;—to Controversies to which the United States shall be a Party;—to Controversies between two or more States;—between a State and Citizens of another State,—between Citizens of different States,—between Citizens of the same State claiming Lands under Grants of different States, and between a State, or the Citizens thereof, and foreign States, Citizens or Subjects.

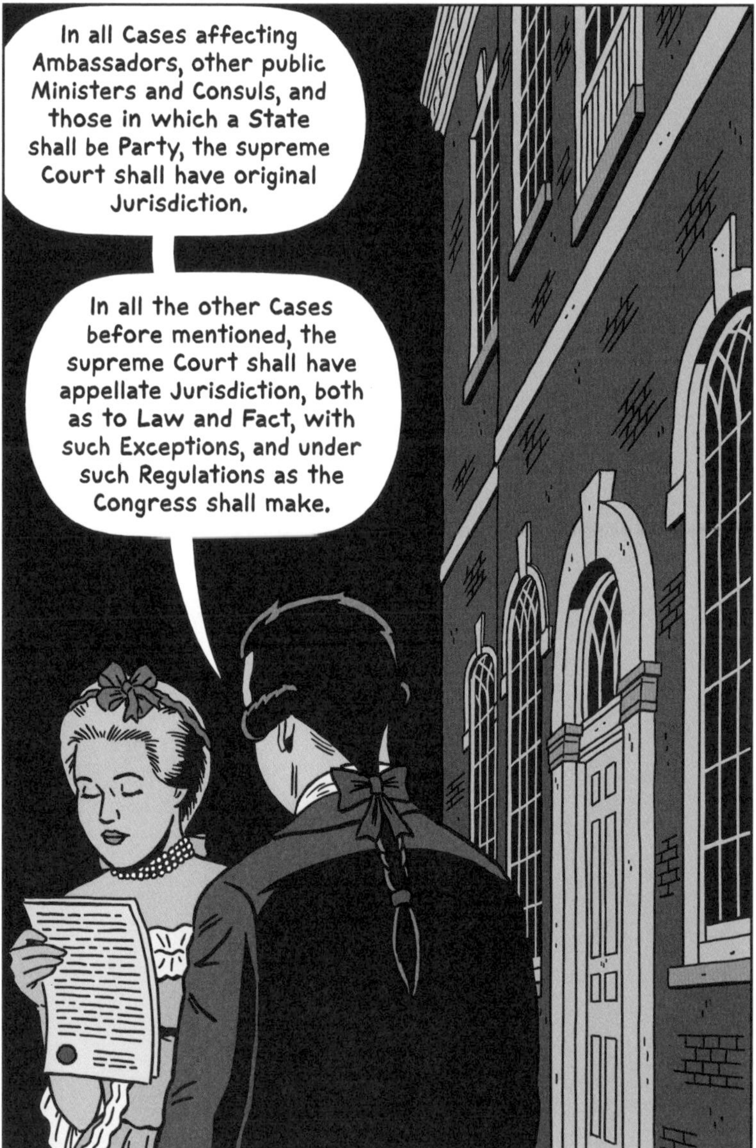
In all Cases affecting Ambassadors, other public Ministers and Consuls, and those in which a State shall be Party, the supreme Court shall have original Jurisdiction.
In all the other Cases before mentioned, the supreme Court shall have appellate Jurisdiction, both as to Law and Fact, with such Exceptions, and under such Regulations as the Congress shall make.

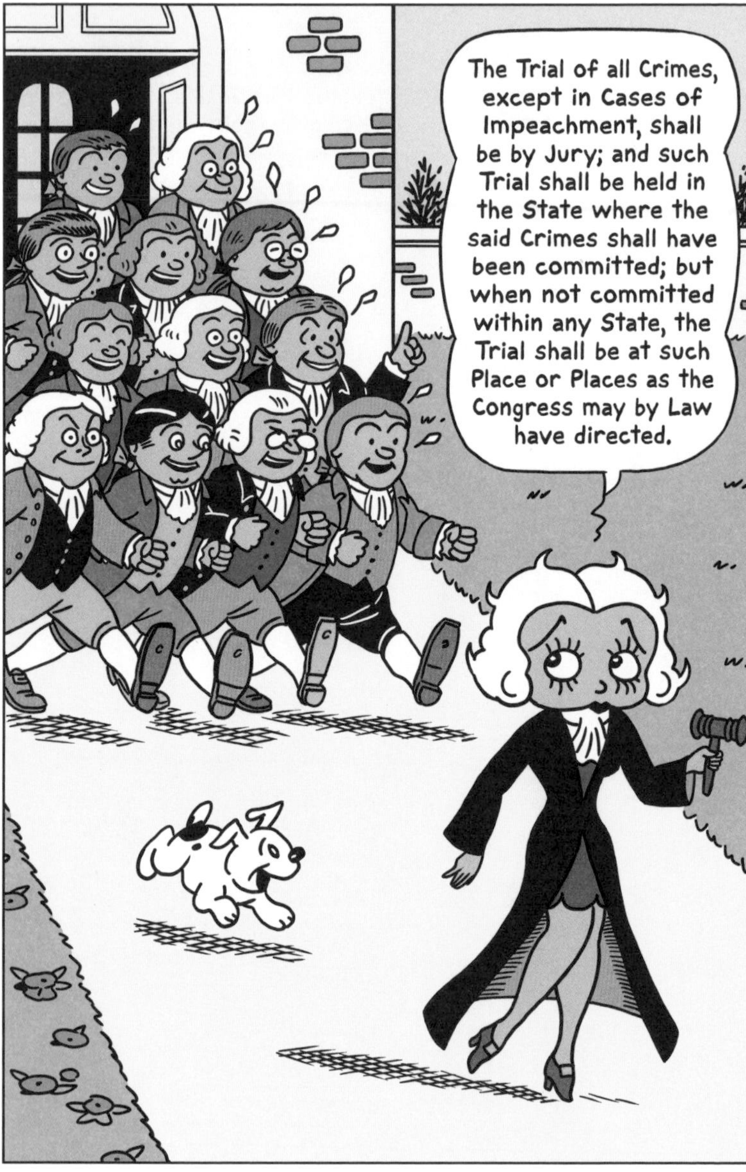
The Trial of all Crimes, except in Cases of Impeachment, shall be by Jury; and such Trial shall be held in the State where the said Crimes shall have been committed; but when not committed within any State, the Trial shall be at such Place or Places as the Congress may by Law have directed.

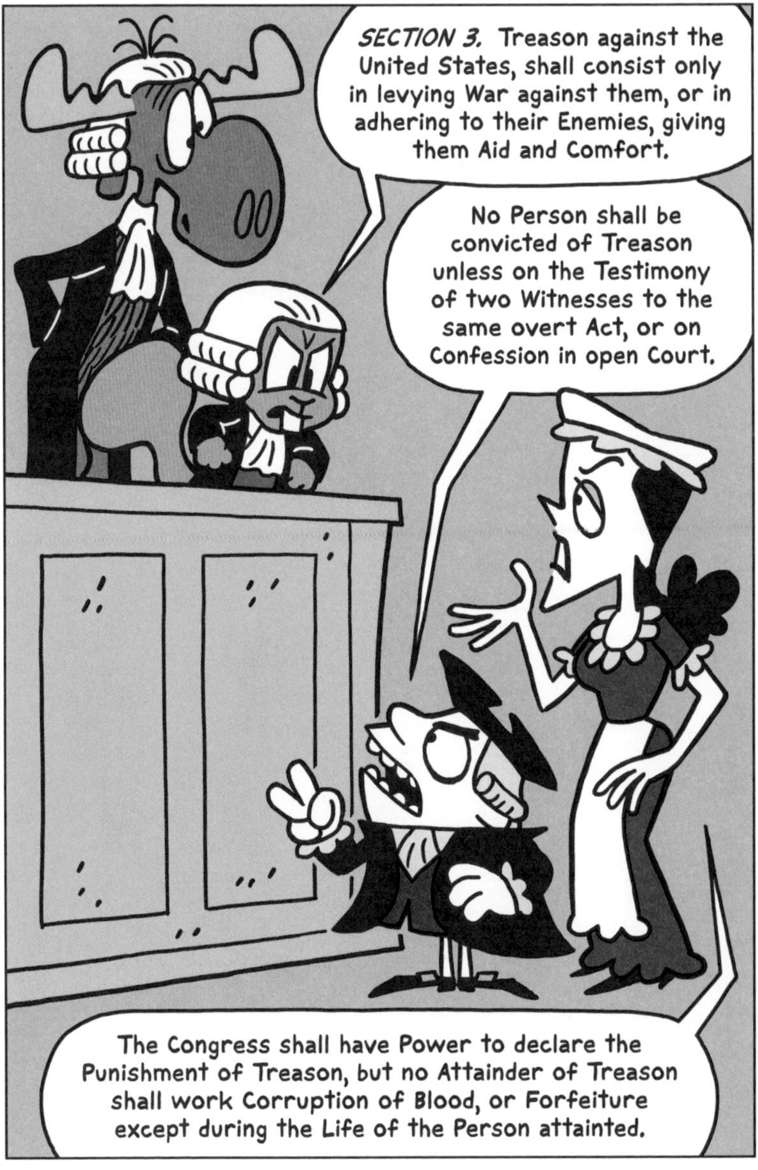
SECTION 3. Treason against the United States, shall consist only in levying War against them, or in adhering to their Enemies, giving them Aid and Comfort.
No Person shall be convicted of Treason unless on the Testimony of two Witnesses to the same overt Act, or on Confession in open Court.
The Congress shall have Power to declare the Punishment of Treason, but no Attainder of Treason shall work Corruption of Blood, or Forfeiture except during the Life of the Person attainted.

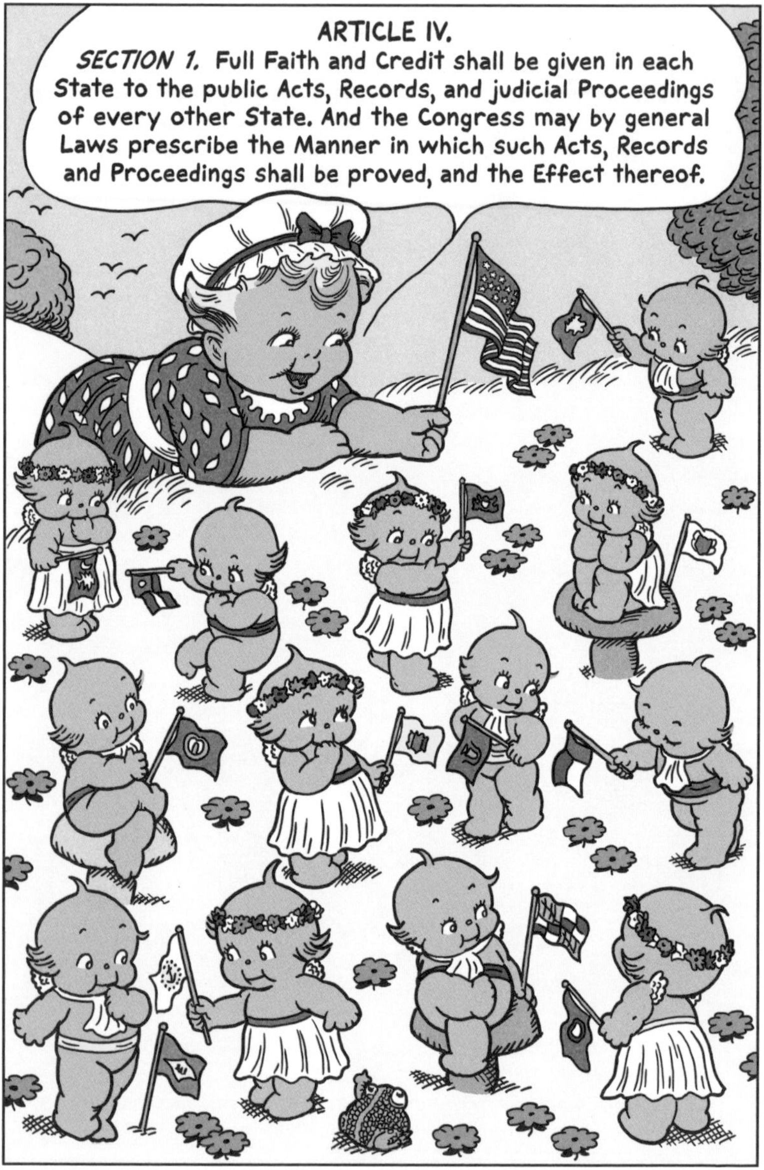
ARTICLE IV.
SECTION 1. Full Faith and Credit shall be given in each State to the public Acts, Records, and judicial Proceedings of every other State. And the Congress may by general Laws prescribe the Manner in which such Acts, Records and Proceedings shall be proved, and the Effect thereof.

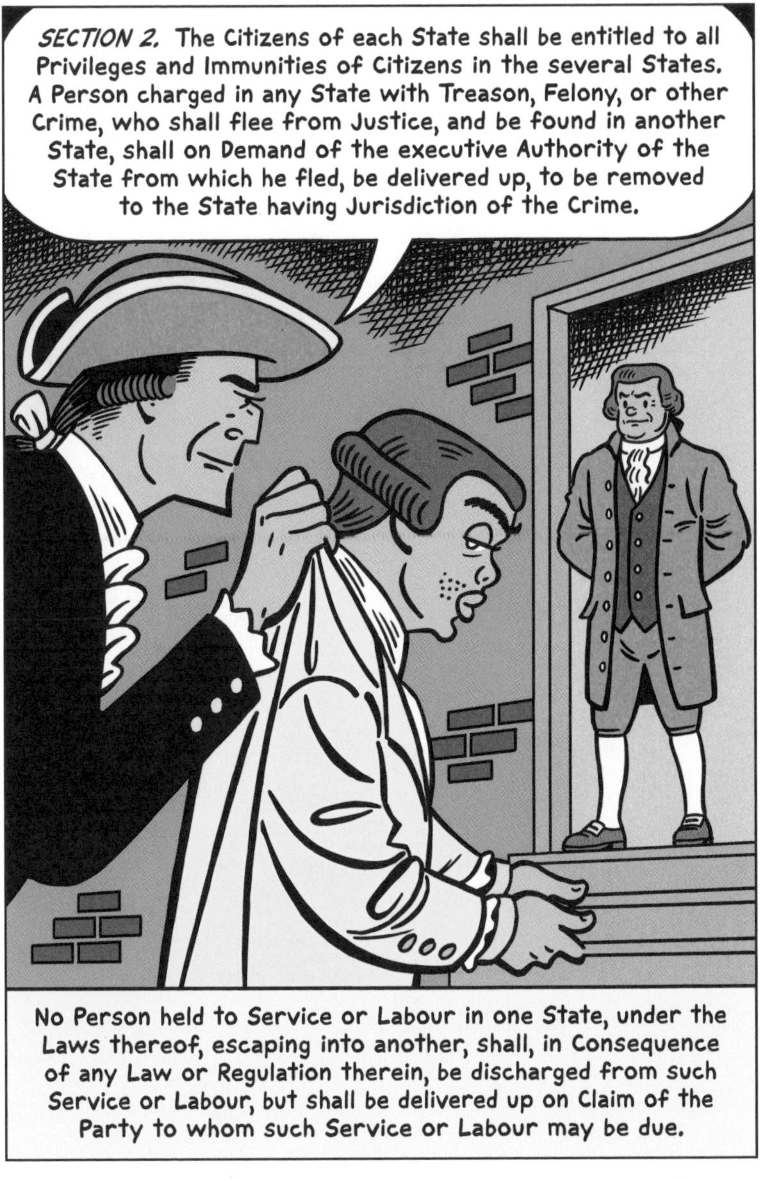
SECTION 2. The Citizens of each State shall be entitled to all Privileges and Immunities of Citizens in the several States. A Person charged in any State with Treason, Felony, or other Crime, who shall flee from Justice, and be found in another State, shall on Demand of the executive Authority of the State from which he fled, be delivered up, to be removed to the State having Jurisdiction of the Crime.
No Person held to Service or Labour in one State, under the Laws thereof, escaping into another, shall, in Consequence of any Law or Regulation therein, be discharged from such Service or Labour, but shall be delivered up on Claim of the Party to whom such Service or Labour may be due.

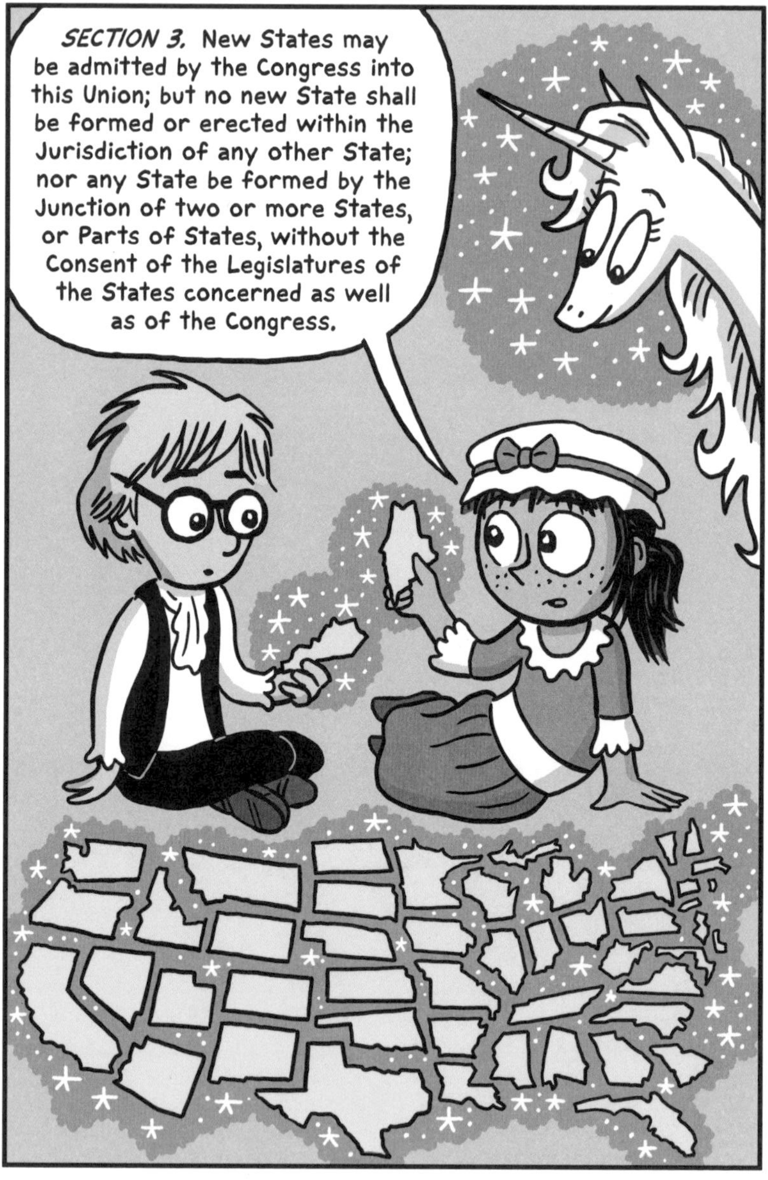
SECTION 3. New States may be admitted by the Congress into this Union; but no new State shall be formed or erected within the Jurisdiction of any other State; nor any State be formed by the Junction of two or more States, or Parts of States, without the Consent of the Legislatures of the States concerned as well as of the Congress.

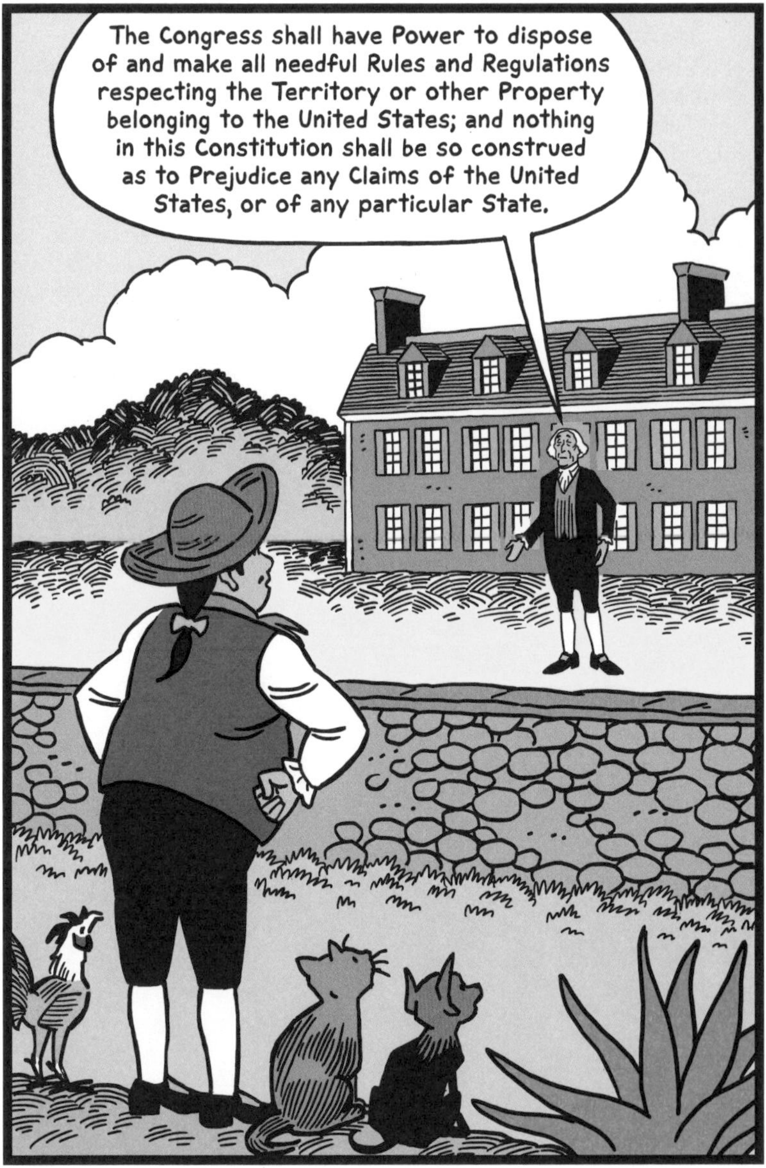
The Congress shall have Power to dispose of and make all needful Rules and Regulations respecting the Territory or other Property belonging to the United States; and nothing in this Constitution shall be so construed as to Prejudice any Claims of the United States, or of any particular State.

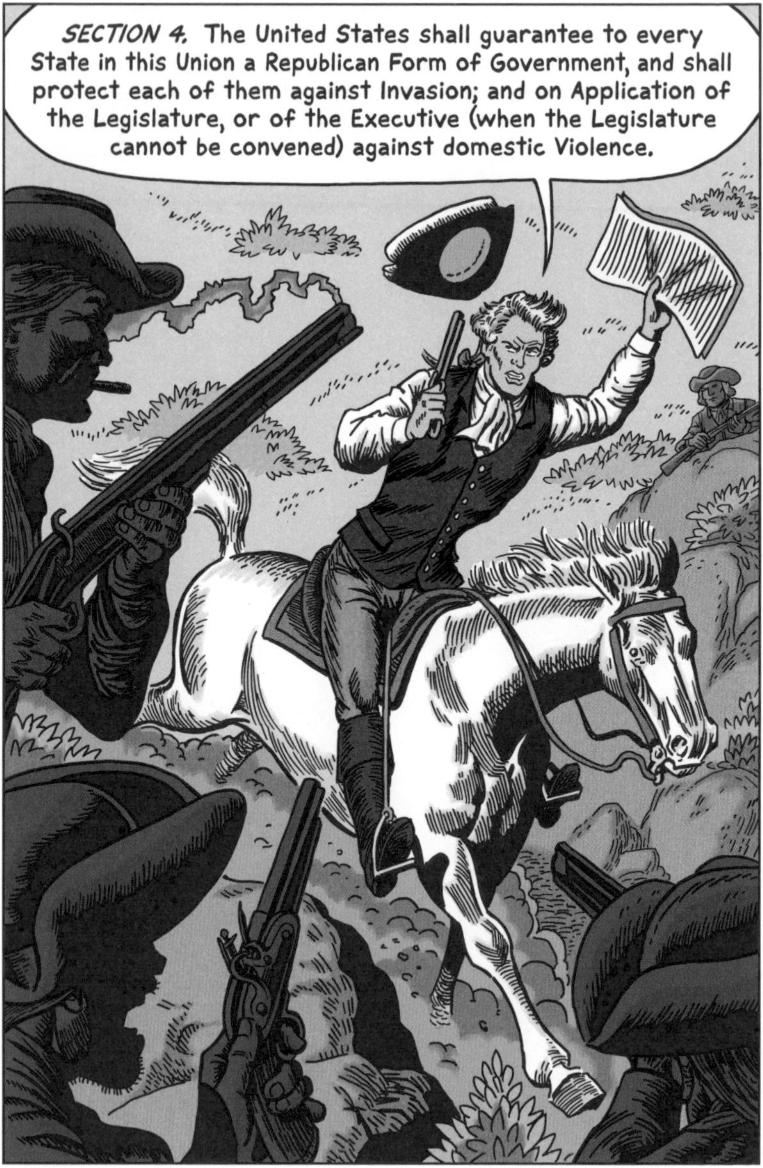
SECTION 4. The United States shall guarantee to every State in this Union a Republican Form of Government, and shall protect each of them against Invasion; and on Application of the Legislature, or of the Executive (when the Legislature cannot be convened) against domestic Violence.

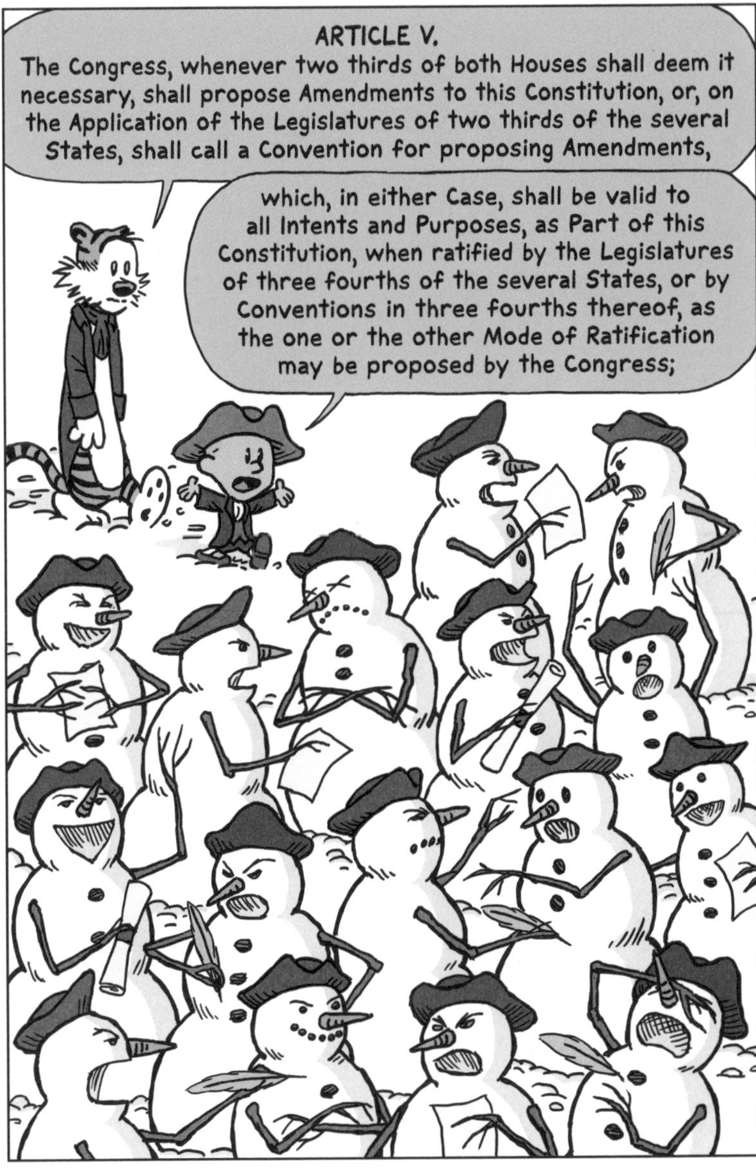
ARTICLE V.
The Congress, whenever two thirds of both Houses shall deem it necessary, shall propose Amendments to this Constitution, or, on the Application of the Legislatures of two thirds of the several States, shall call a Convention for proposing Amendments,
which, in either Case, shall be valid to all Intents and Purposes, as Part of this Constitution, when ratified by the Legislatures of three fourths of the several States, or by Conventions in three fourths thereof, as the one or the other Mode of Ratification may be proposed by the Congress;

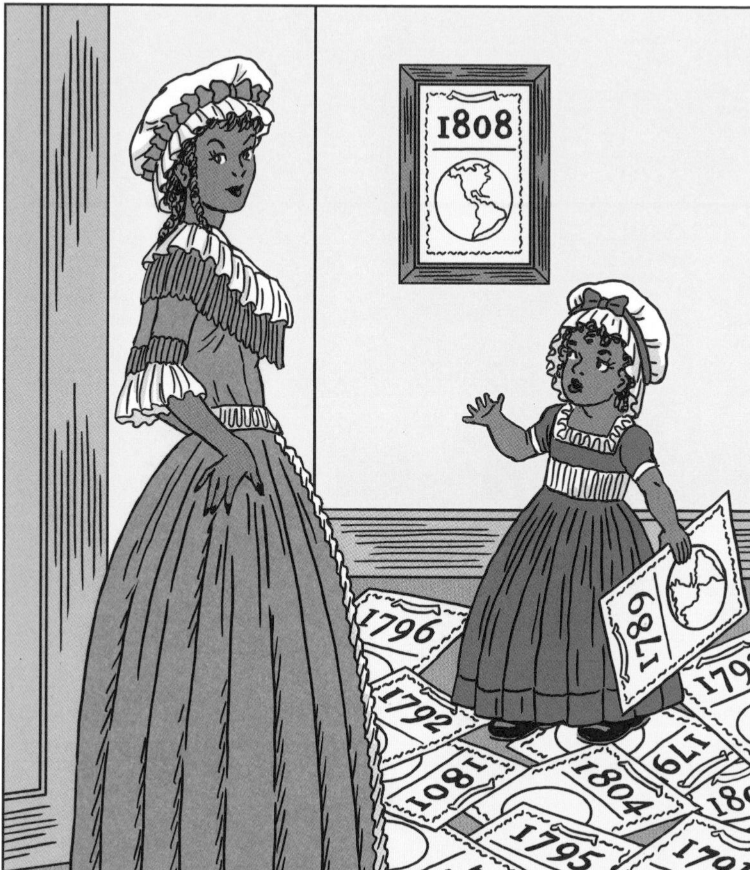
1808
1796
1789
1792
1804
1801
1795
1791
1790
1794
1805
1802
1803
1798

Provided that no Amendment which may be made prior to the Year One thousand eight hundred and eight shall in any Manner affect the first and fourth Clauses in the Ninth Section of the first Article; and that no State, without its Consent, shall be deprived of its equal Suffrage in the Senate.

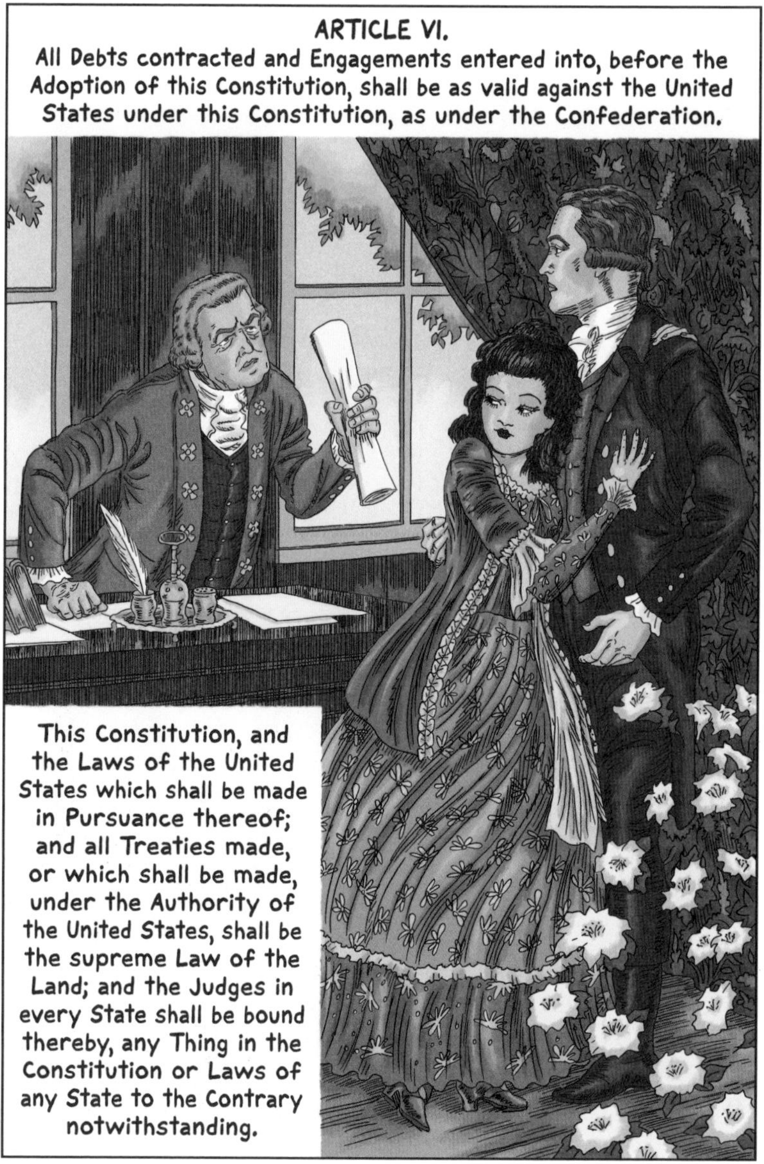
ARTICLE VI.
All Debts contracted and Engagements entered into, before the Adoption of this Constitution, shall be as valid against the United States under this Constitution, as under the Confederation.
This Constitution, and the Laws of the United States which shall be made in Pursuance thereof; and all Treaties made, or which shall be made, under the Authority of the United States, shall be the supreme Law of the Land; and the Judges in every State shall be bound thereby, any Thing in the Constitution or Laws of any State to the Contrary notwithstanding.

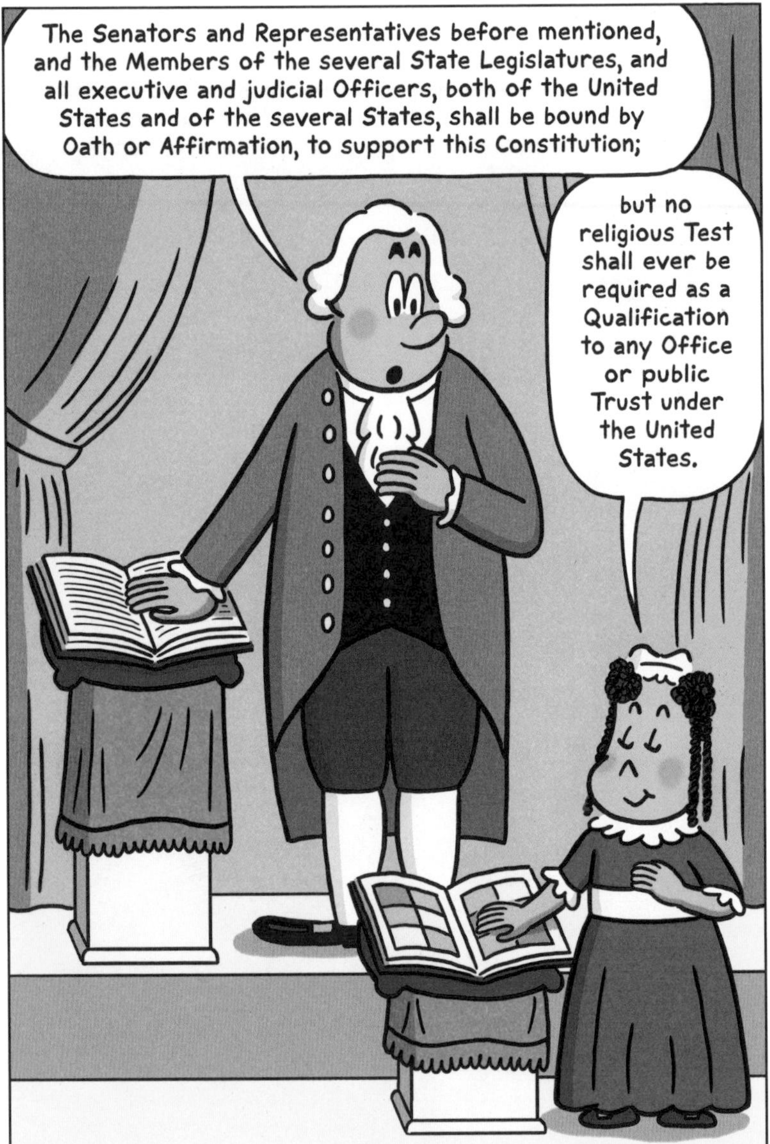
The Senators and Representatives before mentioned, and the Members of the several State Legislatures, and all executive and judicial Officers, both of the United States and of the several States, shall be bound by Oath or Affirmation, to support this Constitution;
but no religious Test shall ever be required as a Qualification to any Office or public Trust under the United States.

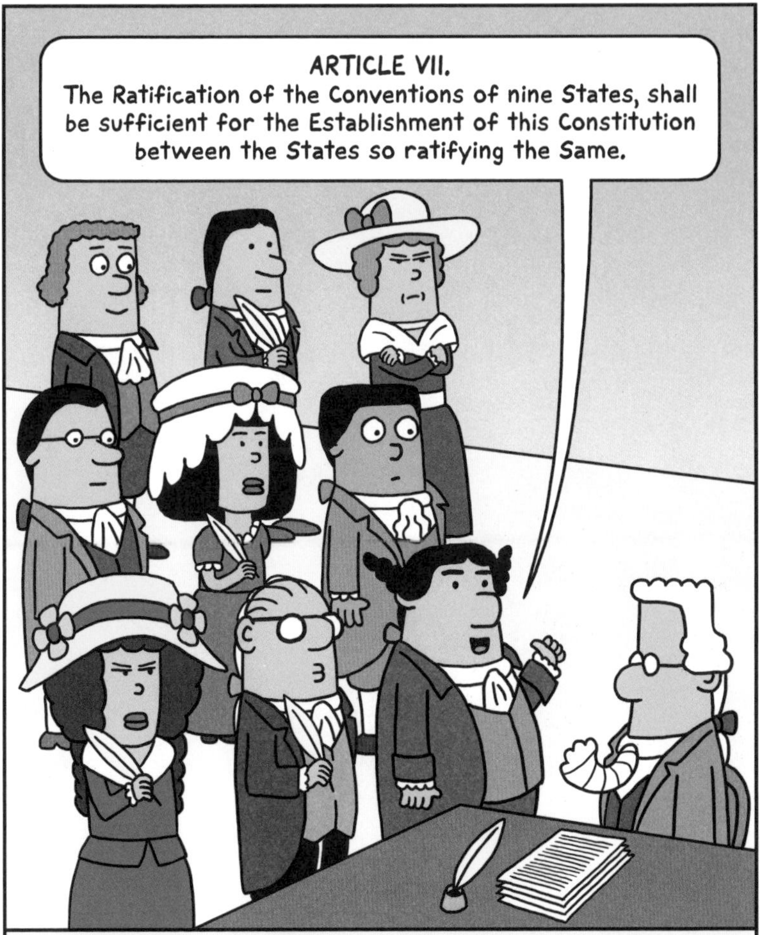
ARTICLE VII.
The Ratification of the Conventions of nine States, shall be sufficient for the Establishment of this Constitution between the States so ratifying the Same.

The Word, "the," being interlined between the seventh and eighth Lines of the first Page, The Word "Thirty" being partly written on an Erazure in the fifteenth Line of the first Page, The Words "is tried" being interlined between the thirty second and thirty third Lines of the first Page and the Word "the" being interlined between the forty third and forty fourth Lines of the second Page. Attest WILLIAM JACKSON Secretary

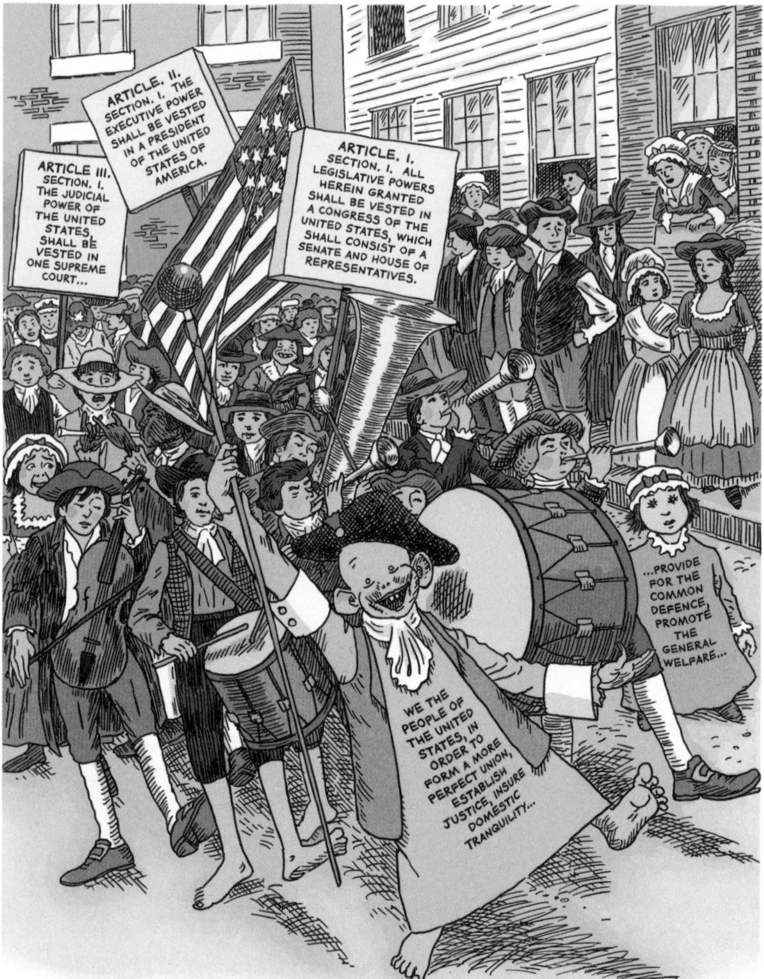
ARTICLE III. SECTION. I. THE JUDICIAL POWER OF THE UNITED STATES, SHALL BE VESTED IN ONE SUPREME COURT...
ARTICLE. II. SECTION. I. THE EXECUTIVE POWER SHALL BE VESTED IN A PRESIDENT OF THE UNITED STATES OF AMERICA.
ARTICLE. I. SECTION. I. ALL LEGISLATIVE POWERS HEREIN GRANTED SHALL BE VESTED IN A CONGRESS OF THE UNITED STATES, WHICH SHALL CONSIST OF A SENATE AND HOUSE OF REPRESENTATIVES.
...PROVIDE FOR THE COMMON DEFENCE, PROMOTE THE GENERAL WELFARE...
WE THE PEOPLE OF THE UNITED STATES, IN ORDER TO FORM A MORE PERFECT UNION, ESTABLISH JUSTICE, INSURE DOMESTIC TRANQUILITY...

done in Convention by the Unanimous Consent of the States present the Seventeenth Day of September in the Year of our Lord one thousand seven hundred and Eighty seven and of the Independence of the United States of America the Twelfth In Witness whereof We have hereunto subscribed our Names,

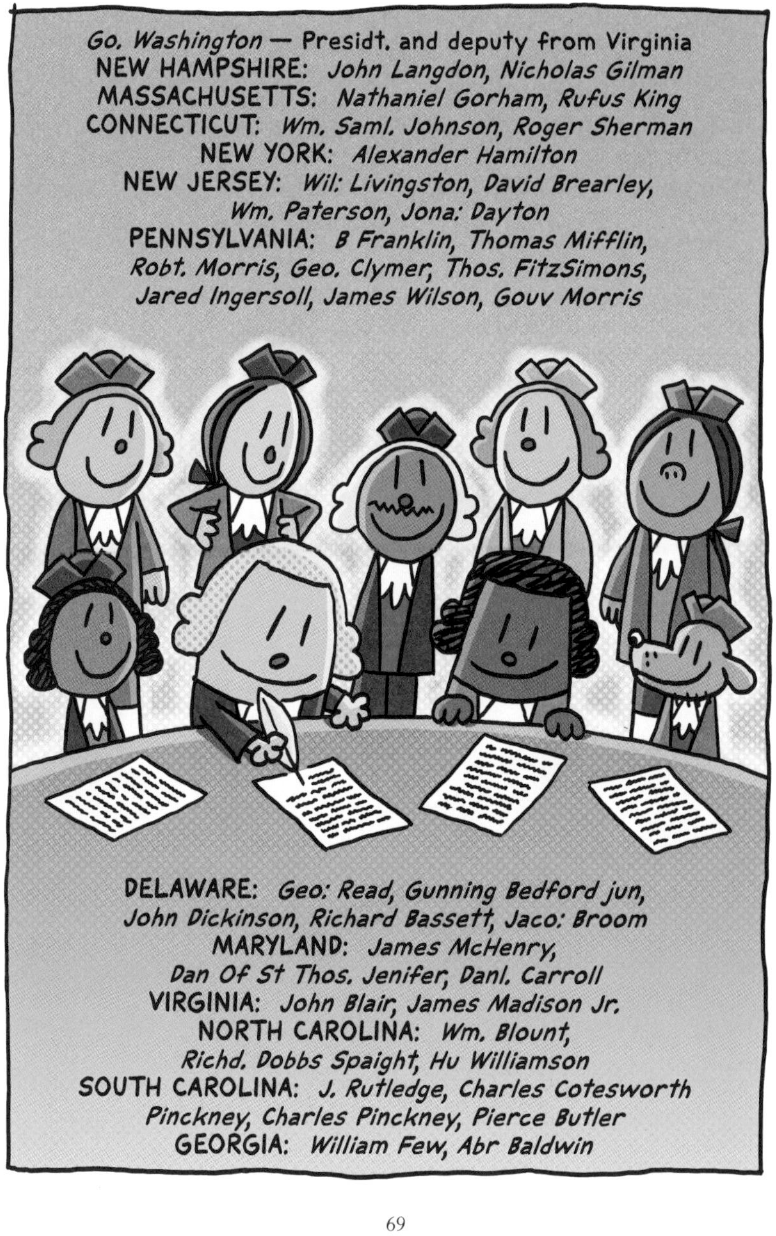
Go. Washington — Presidt. and deputy from Virginia
NEW HAMPSHIRE: John Langdon, Nicholas Gilman
MASSACHUSETTS: Nathaniel Gorham, Rufus King
CONNECTICUT: Wm. Saml. Johnson, Roger Sherman
NEW YORK: Alexander Hamilton
NEW JERSEY: Wil: Livingston, David Brearley, Wm. Paterson, Jona: Dayton
PENNSYLVANIA: B Franklin, Thomas Mifflin, Robt. Morris, Geo. Clymer, Thos. FitzSimons, Jared Ingersoll, James Wilson, Gouv Morris
DELAWARE: Geo: Read, Gunning Bedford jun, John Dickinson, Richard Bassett, Jaco: Broom
MARYLAND: James McHenry, Dan Of St Thos. Jenifer, Danl. Carroll
VIRGINIA: John Blair, James Madison Jr.
NORTH CAROLINA: Wm. Blount, Richd. Dobbs Spaight, Hu Williamson
SOUTH CAROLINA: J. Rutledge, Charles Cotesworth Pinckney, Charles Pinckney, Pierce Butler
GEORGIA: William Few, Abr Baldwin

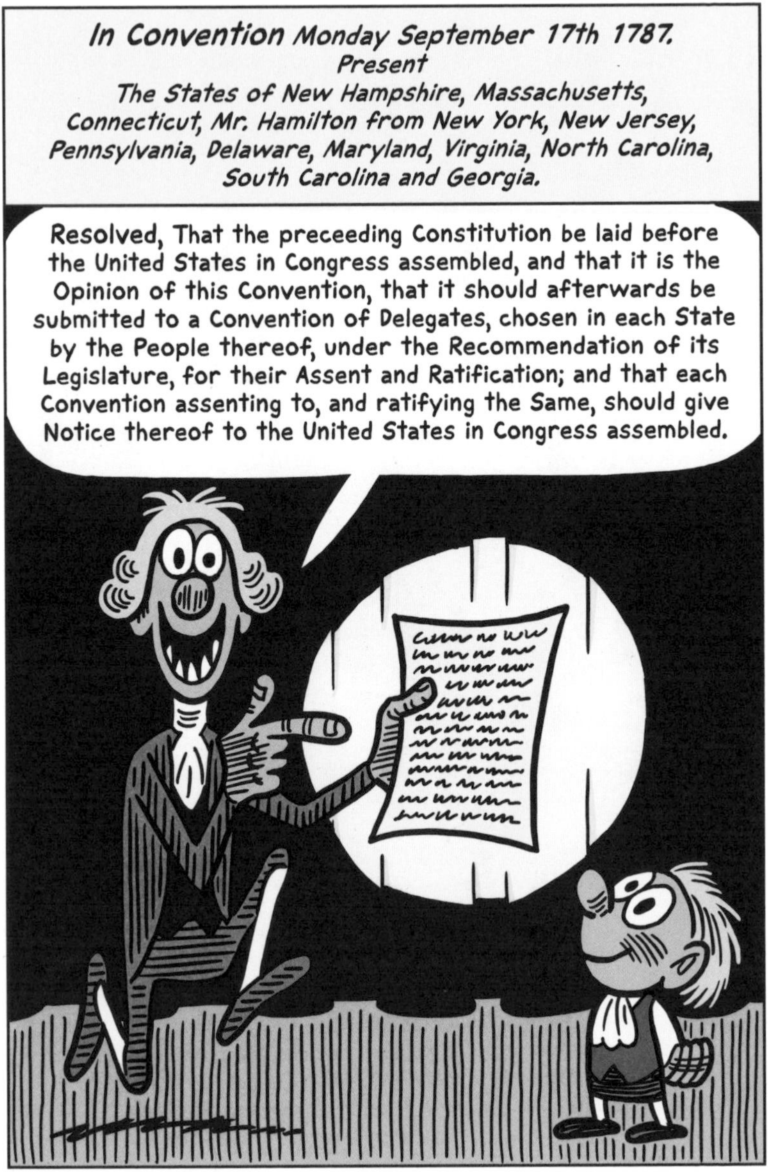
In Convention Monday September 17th 1787.
Present
The States of New Hampshire, Massachusetts, Connecticut, Mr. Hamilton from New York, New Jersey, Pennsylvania, Delaware, Maryland, Virginia, North Carolina, South Carolina and Georgia.
Resolved, That the preceeding Constitution be laid before the United States in Congress assembled, and that it is the Opinion of this Convention, that it should afterwards be submitted to a Convention of Delegates, chosen in each State by the People thereof, under the Recommendation of its Legislature, for their Assent and Ratification; and that each Convention assenting to, and ratifying the Same, should give Notice thereof to the United States in Congress assembled.

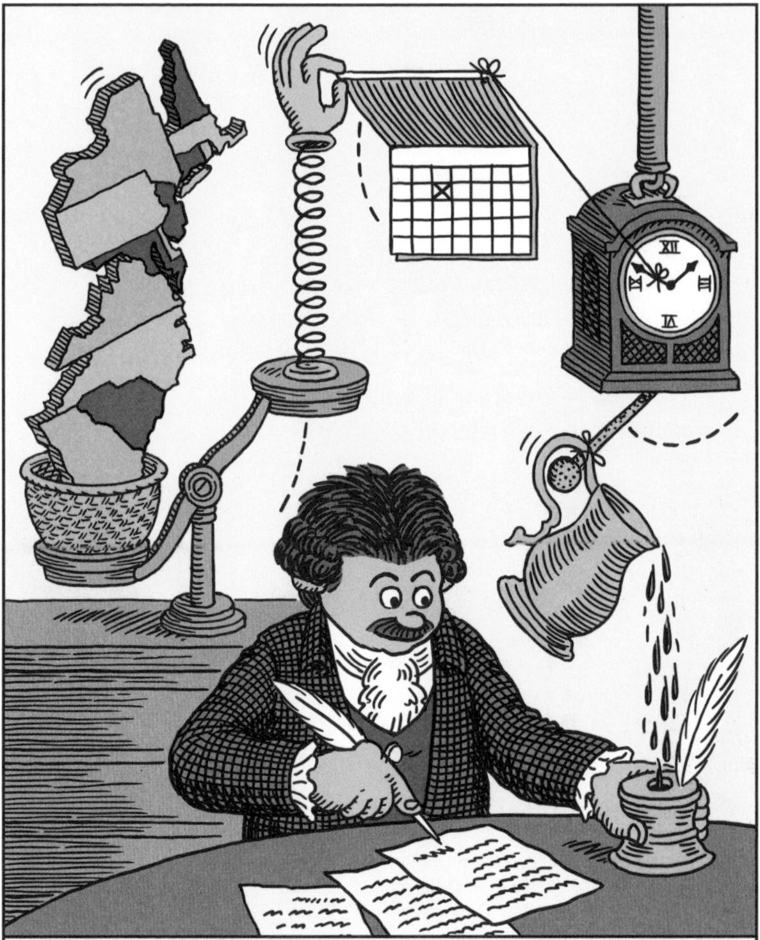

Resolved, That it is the Opinion of this Convention, that as soon as the Conventions of nine States shall have ratified this Constitution, the United States in Congress assembled should fix a Day on which Electors should be appointed by the States which shall have ratified the same, and a Day on which the Electors should assemble to vote for the President, and the Time and Place for commencing Proceedings under this Constitution.

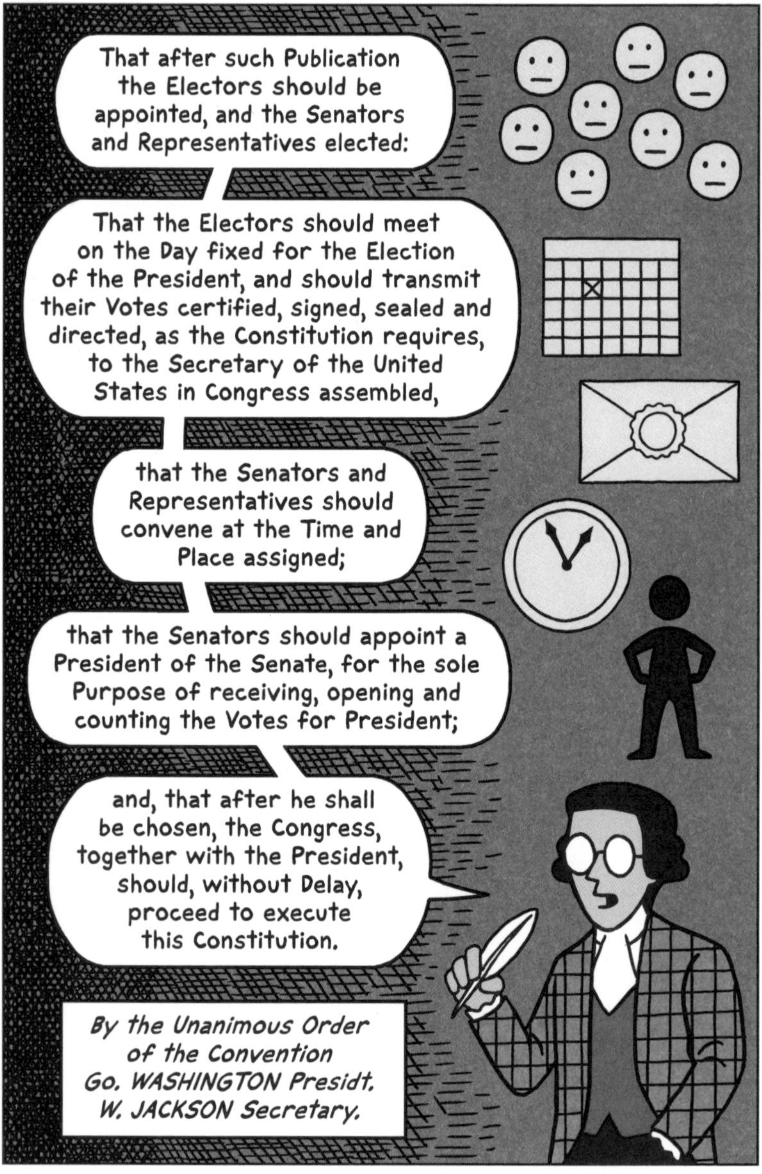
That after such Publication the Electors should be appointed, and the Senators and Representatives elected:
That the Electors should meet on the Day fixed for the Election of the President, and should transmit their Votes certified, signed, sealed and directed, as the Constitution requires, to the Secretary of the United States in Congress assembled,
that the Senators and Representatives should convene at the Time and Place assigned;
that the Senators should appoint a President of the Senate, for the sole Purpose of receiving, opening and counting the Votes for President;
and, that after he shall be chosen, the Congress, together with the President, should, without Delay, proceed to execute this Constitution.
By the Unanimous Order of the Convention
Go. WASHINGTON Presidt.
W. JACKSON Secretary.

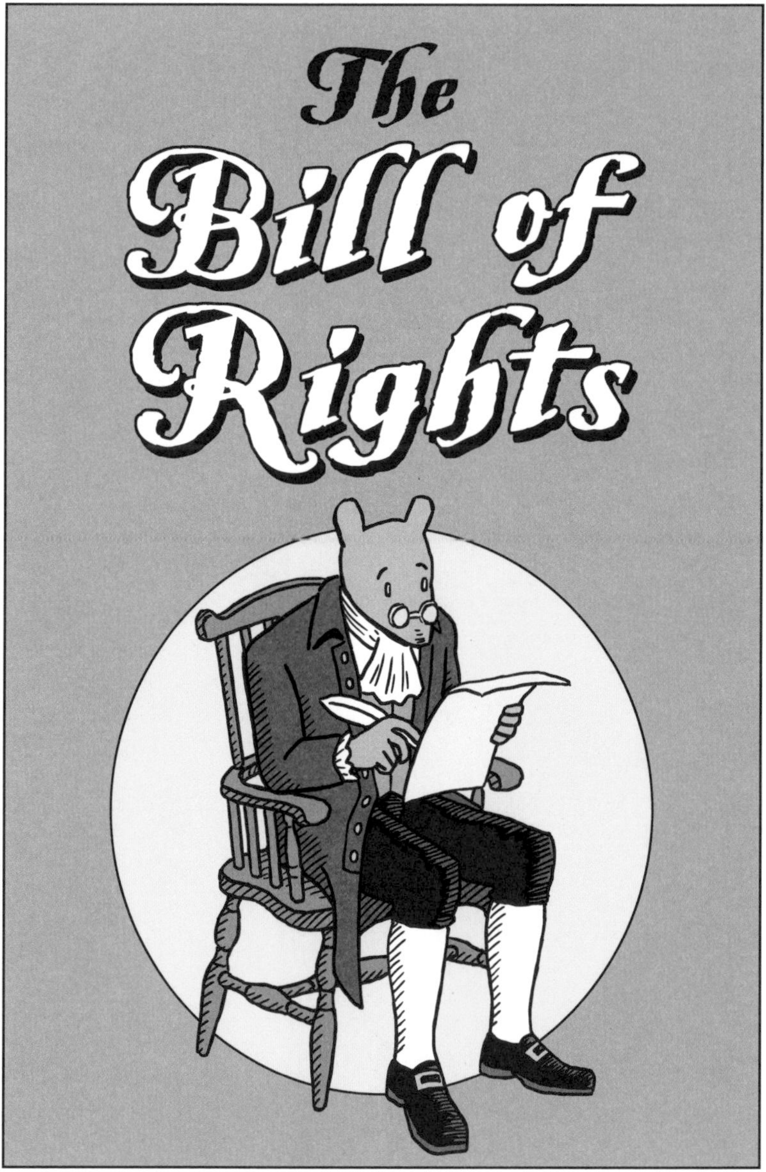
The
Bill of
Rights

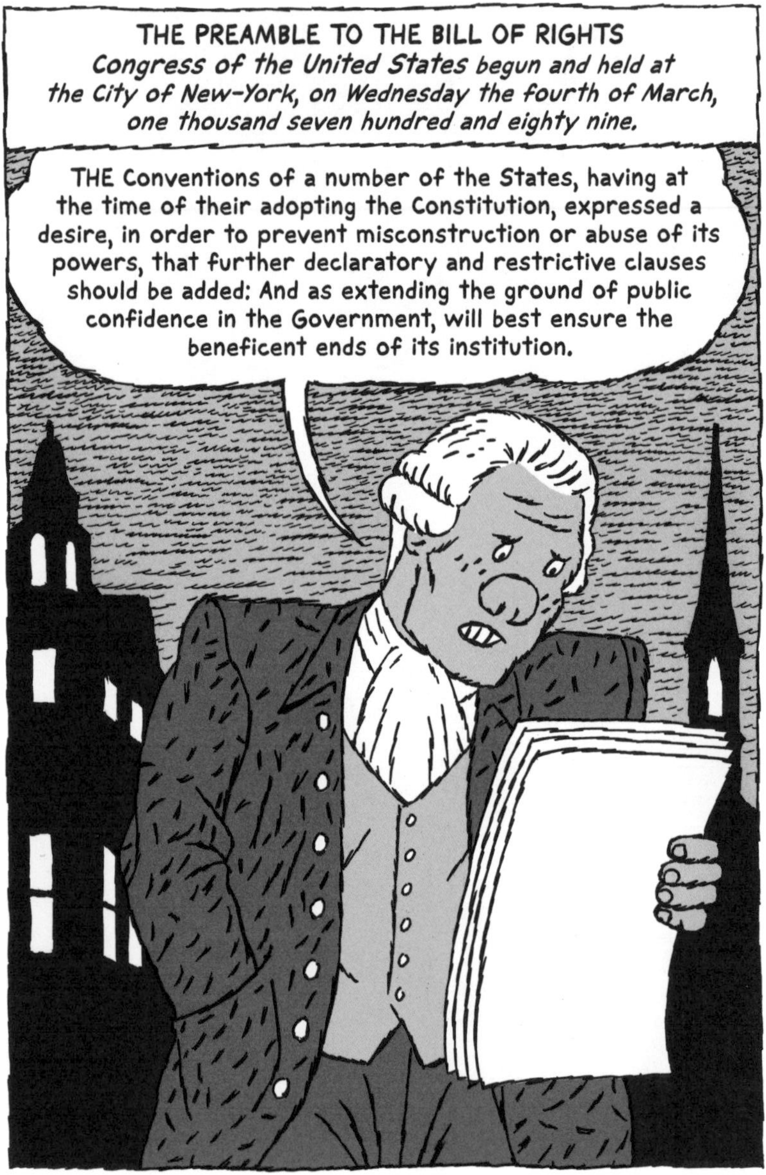
THE PREAMBLE TO THE BILL OF RIGHTS
Congress of the United States begun and held at the City of New-York, on Wednesday the fourth of March, one thousand seven hundred and eighty nine.
THE Conventions of a number of the States, having at the time of their adopting the Constitution, expressed a desire, in order to prevent misconstruction or abuse of its powers, that further declaratory and restrictive clauses should be added: And as extending the ground of public confidence in the Government, will best ensure the beneficent ends of its institution.

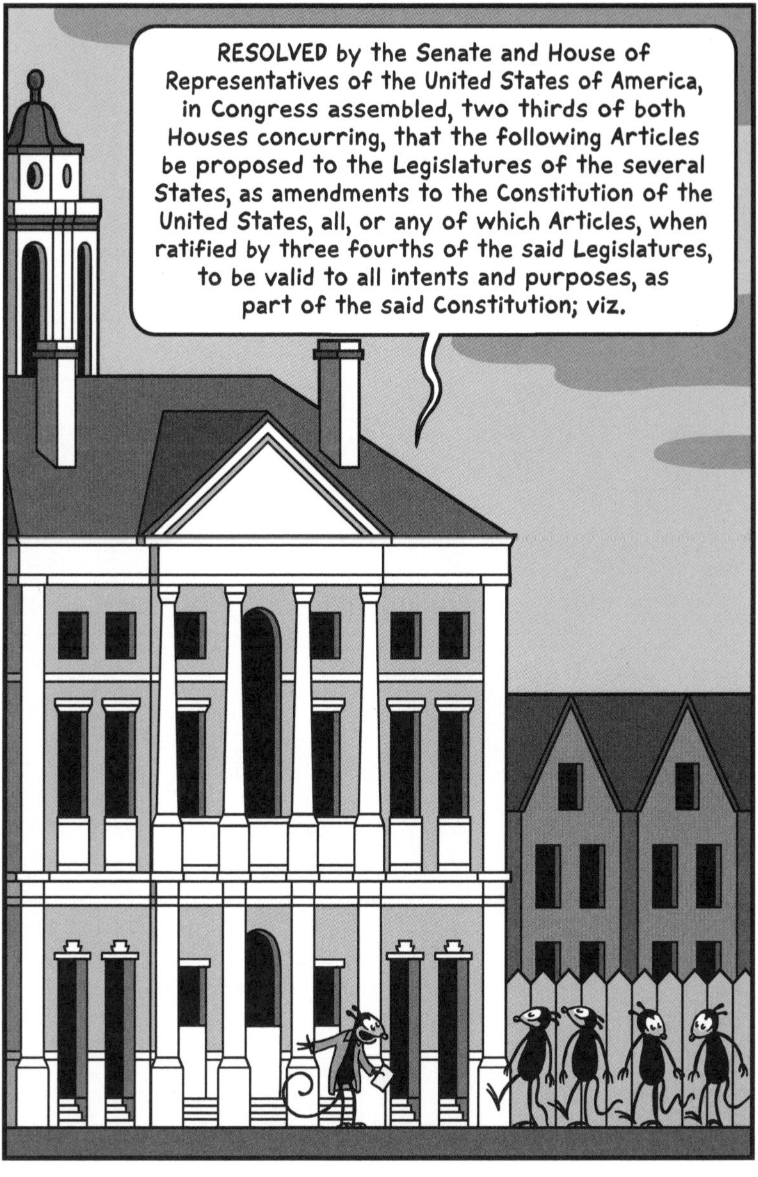
RESOLVED by the Senate and House of Representatives of the United States of America, in Congress assembled, two thirds of both Houses concurring, that the following Articles be proposed to the Legislatures of the several States, as amendments to the Constitution of the United States, all, or any of which Articles, when ratified by three fourths of the said Legislatures, to be valid to all intents and purposes, as part of the said Constitution; viz.

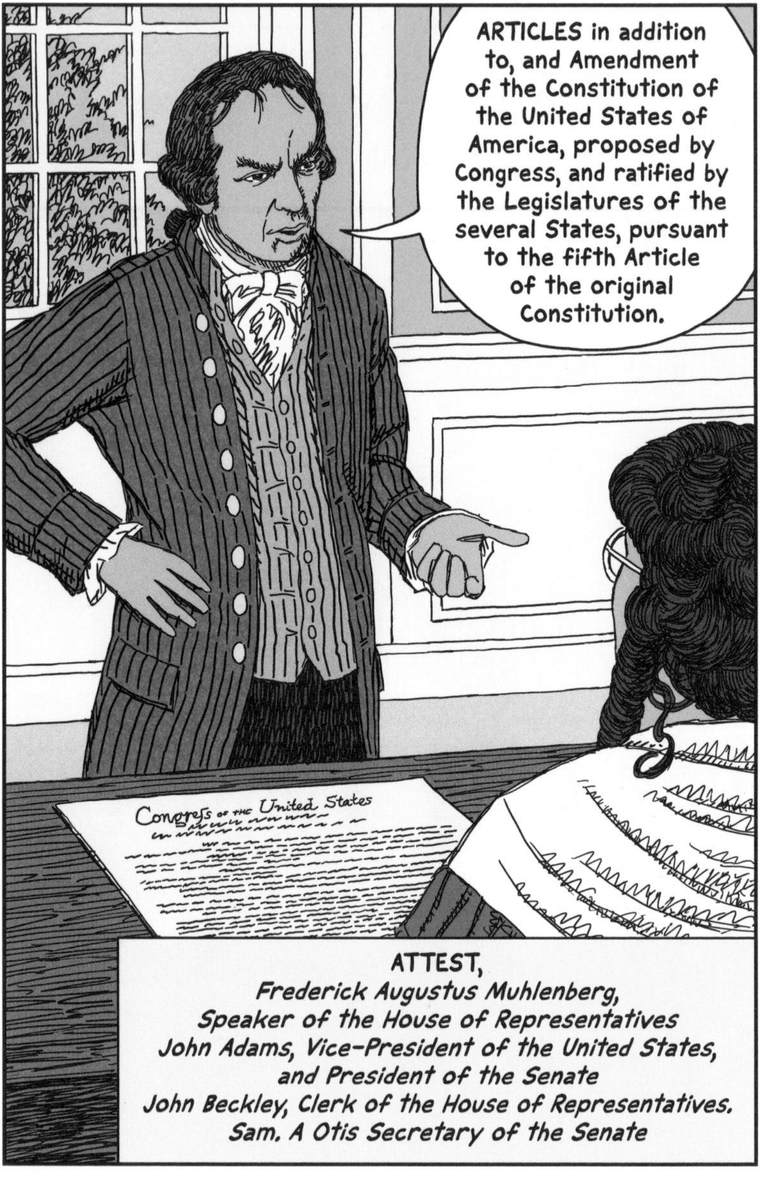
ARTICLES in addition to, and Amendment of the Constitution of the United States of America, proposed by Congress, and ratified by the Legislatures of the several States, pursuant to the fifth Article of the original Constitution.
Congress of the United States
ATTEST,
Frederick Augustus Muhlenberg,
Speaker of the House of Representatives
John Adams, Vice-President of the United States,
and President of the Senate
John Beckley, Clerk of the House of Representatives.
Sam. A Otis Secretary of the Senate

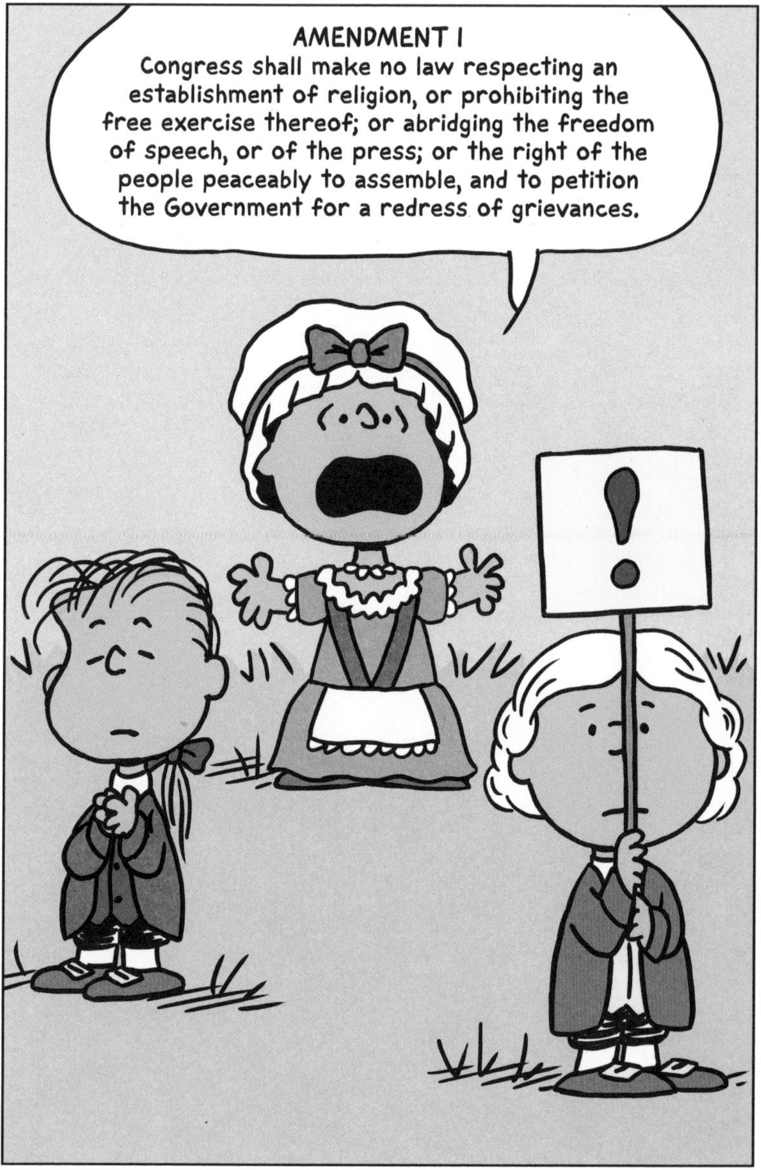
AMENDMENT I
Congress shall make no law respecting an establishment of religion, or prohibiting the free exercise thereof; or abridging the freedom of speech, or of the press; or the right of the people peaceably to assemble, and to petition the Government for a redress of grievances.
!

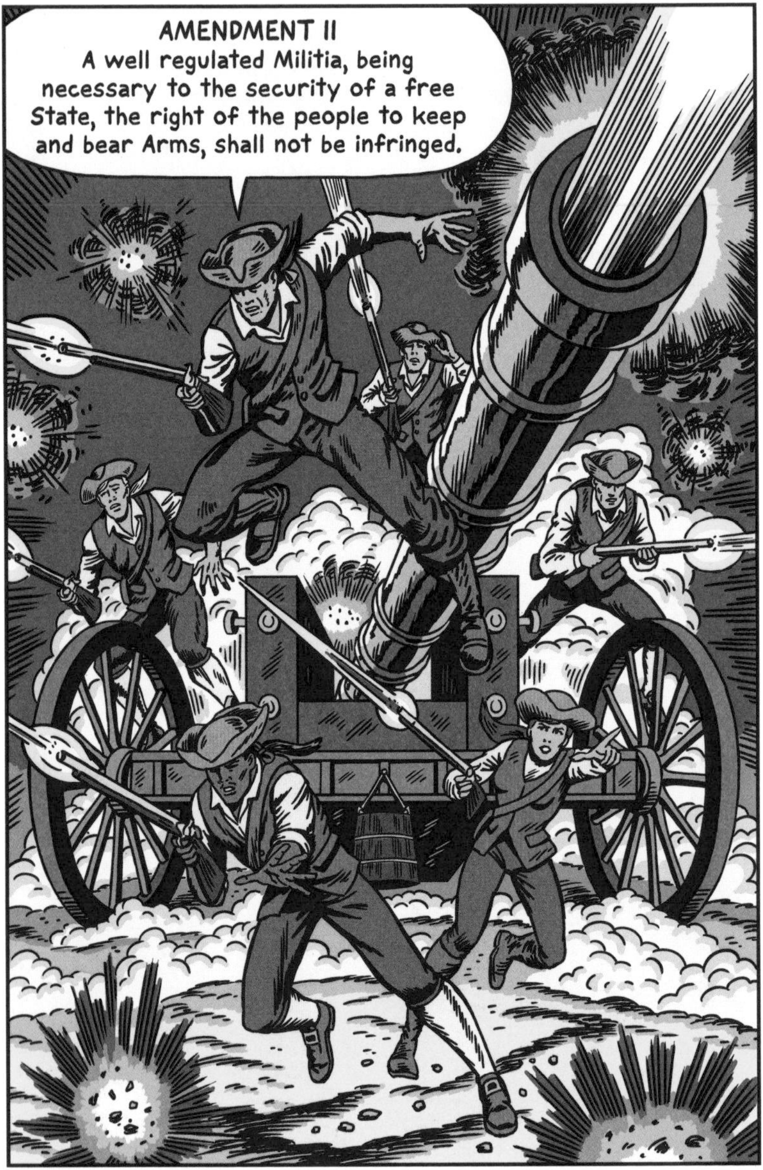
AMENDMENT II
A well regulated Militia, being necessary to the security of a free State, the right of the people to keep and bear Arms, shall not be infringed.

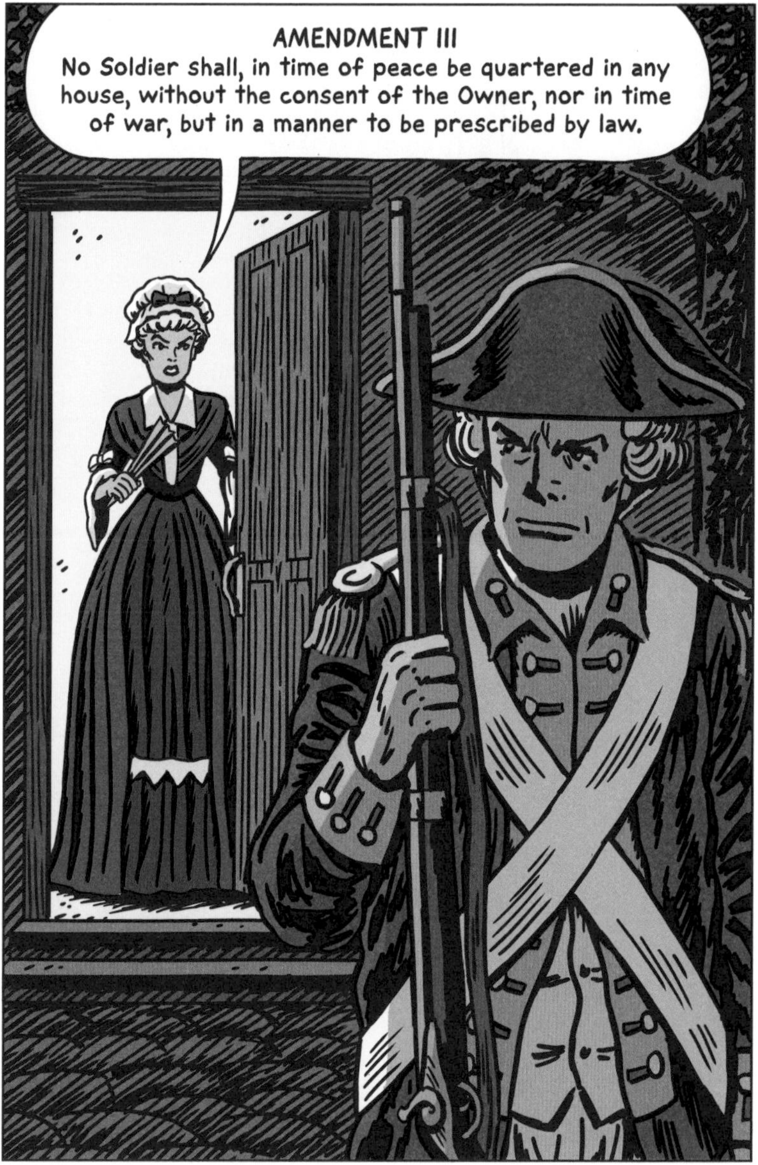
AMENDMENT III
No Soldier shall, in time of peace be quartered in any house, without the consent of the Owner, nor in time of war, but in a manner to be prescribed by law.

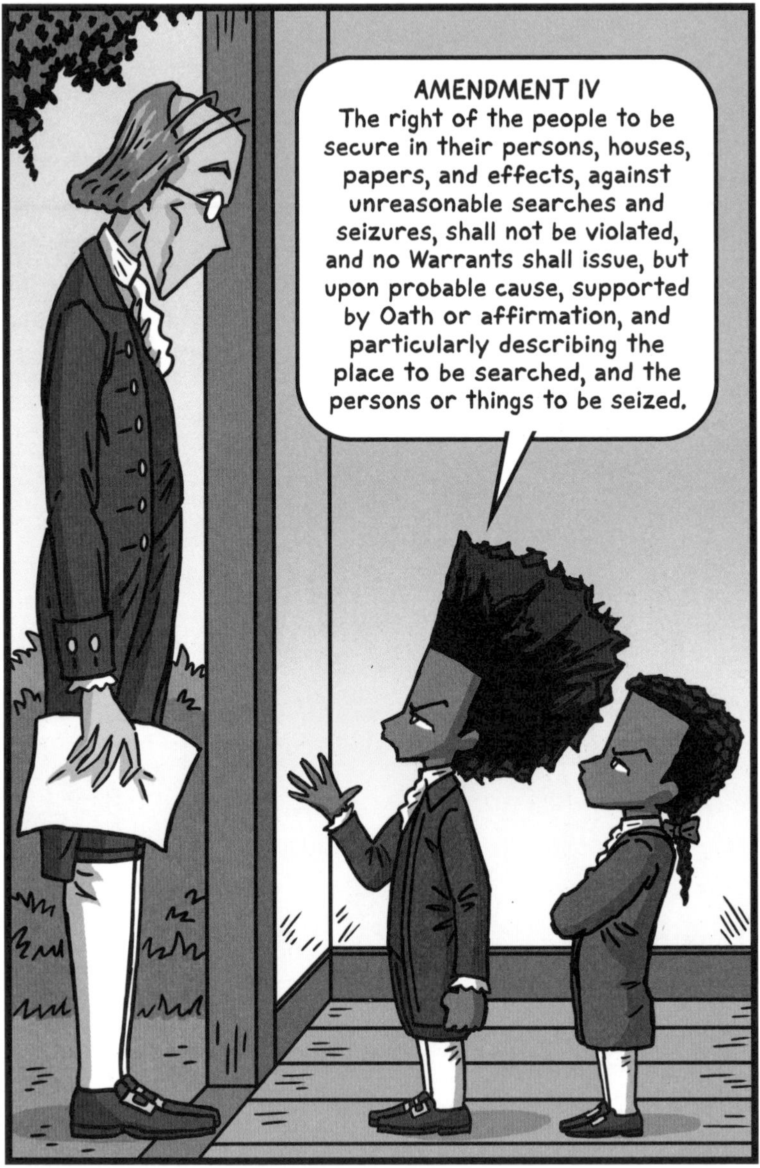
AMENDMENT IV
The right of the people to be secure in their persons, houses, papers, and effects, against unreasonable searches and seizures, shall not be violated, and no Warrants shall issue, but upon probable cause, supported by Oath or affirmation, and particularly describing the place to be searched, and the persons or things to be seized.

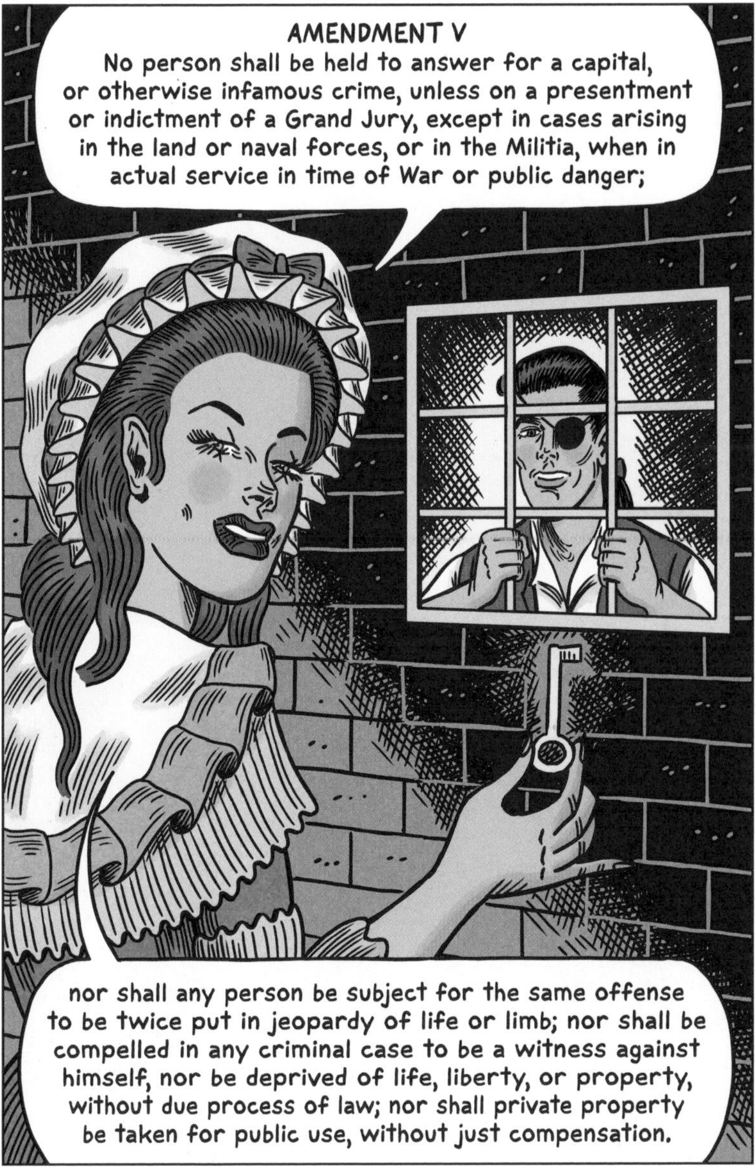
AMENDMENT V
No person shall be held to answer for a capital, or otherwise infamous crime, unless on a presentment or indictment of a Grand Jury, except in cases arising in the land or naval forces, or in the Militia, when in actual service in time of War or public danger;
nor shall any person be subject for the same offense to be twice put in jeopardy of life or limb; nor shall be compelled in any criminal case to be a witness against himself, nor be deprived of life, liberty, or property, without due process of law; nor shall private property be taken for public use, without just compensation.

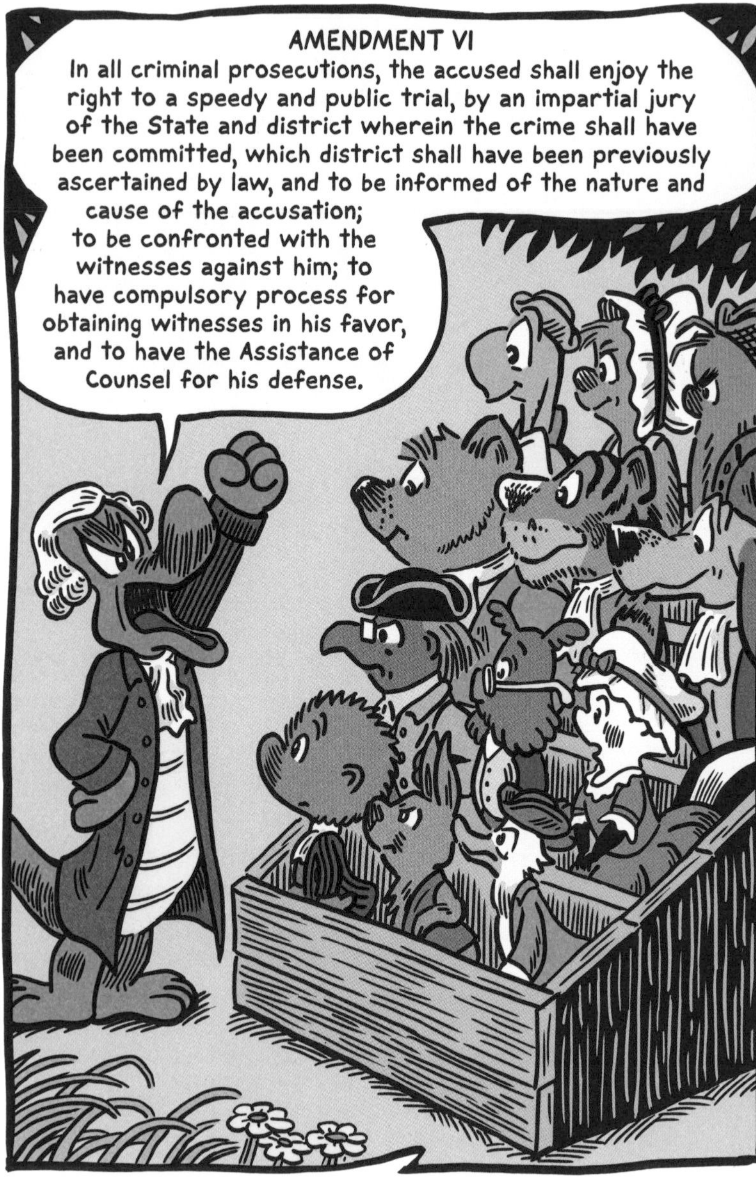
AMENDMENT VI
In all criminal prosecutions, the accused shall enjoy the right to a speedy and public trial, by an impartial jury of the State and district wherein the crime shall have been committed, which district shall have been previously ascertained by law, and to be informed of the nature and cause of the accusation; to be confronted with the witnesses against him; to have compulsory process for obtaining witnesses in his favor, and to have the Assistance of Counsel for his defense.

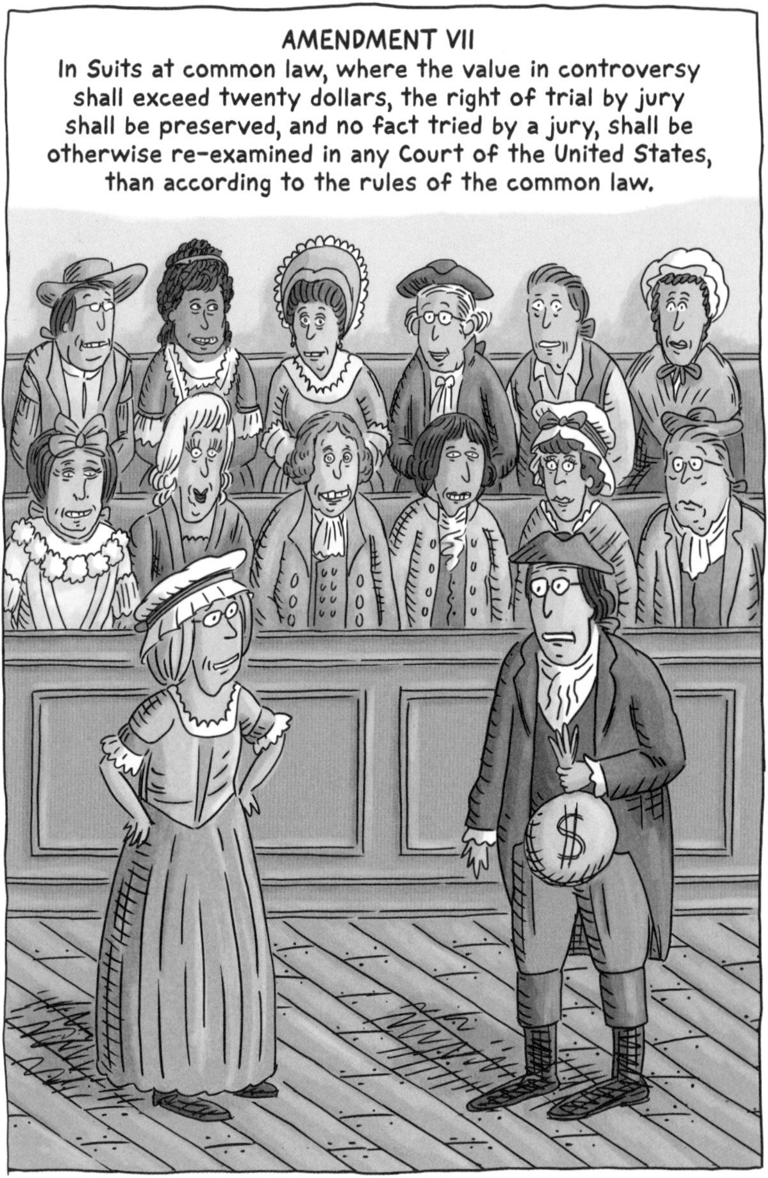
AMENDMENT VII
In Suits at common law, where the value in controversy shall exceed twenty dollars, the right of trial by jury shall be preserved, and no fact tried by a jury, shall be otherwise re-examined in any Court of the United States, than according to the rules of the common law.
$

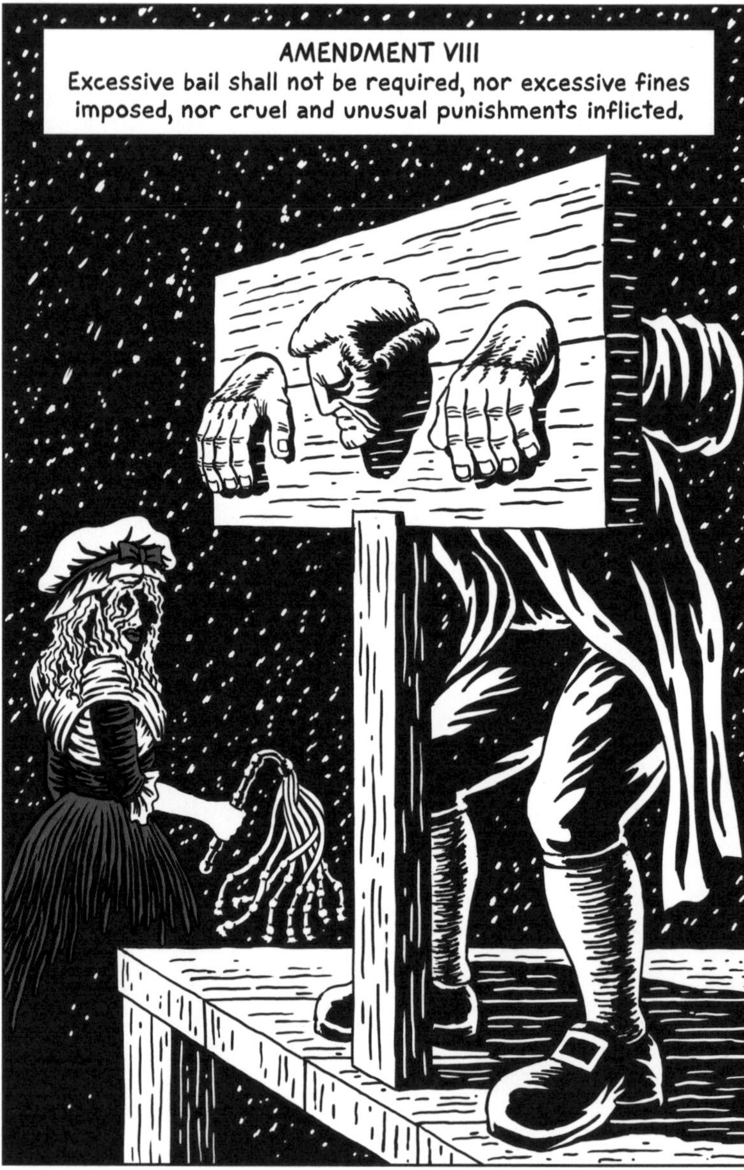
AMENDMENT VIII
Excessive bail shall not be required, nor excessive fines imposed, nor cruel and unusual punishments inflicted.

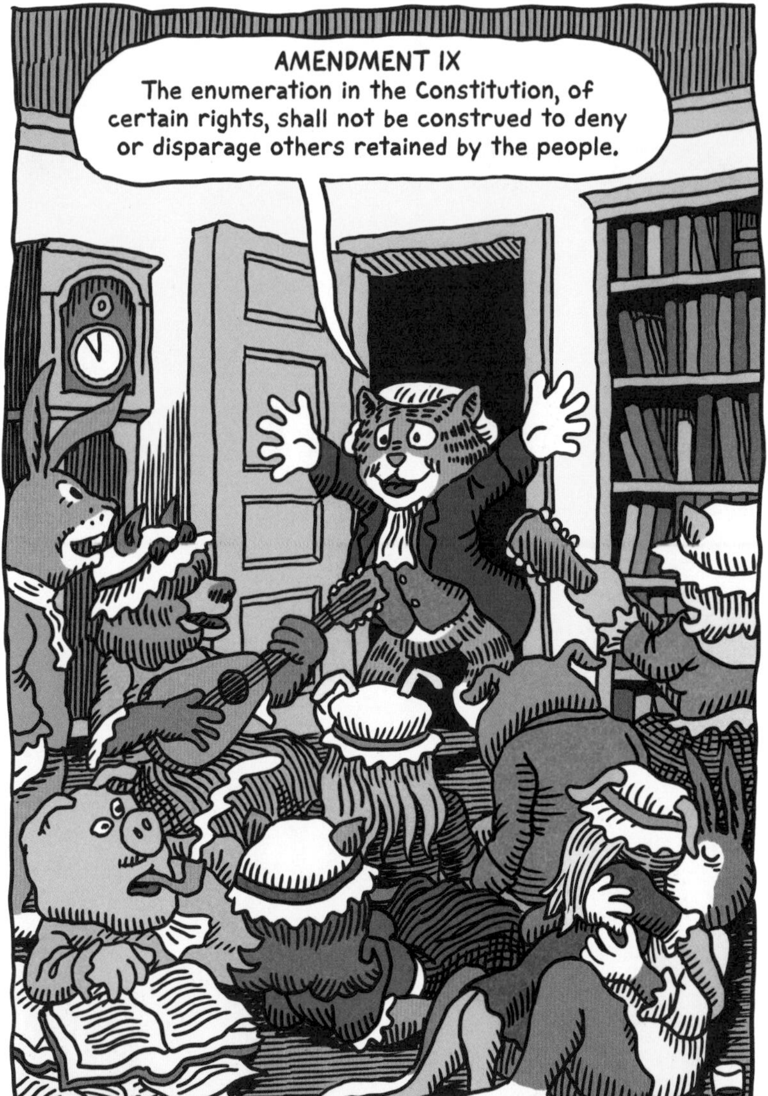
AMENDMENT IX
The enumeration in the Constitution, of certain rights, shall not be construed to deny or disparage others retained by the people.

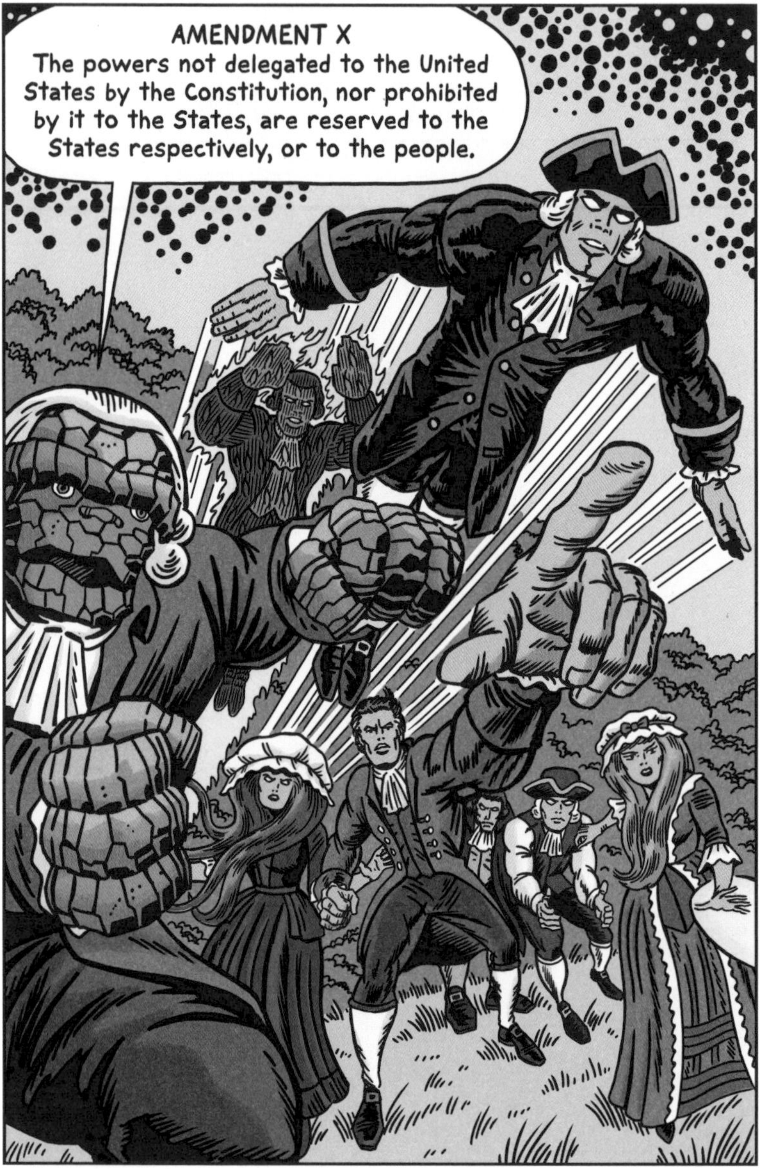
AMENDMENT X
The powers not delegated to the United States by the Constitution, nor prohibited by it to the States, are reserved to the States respectively, or to the people.

The
Additional
Amendments

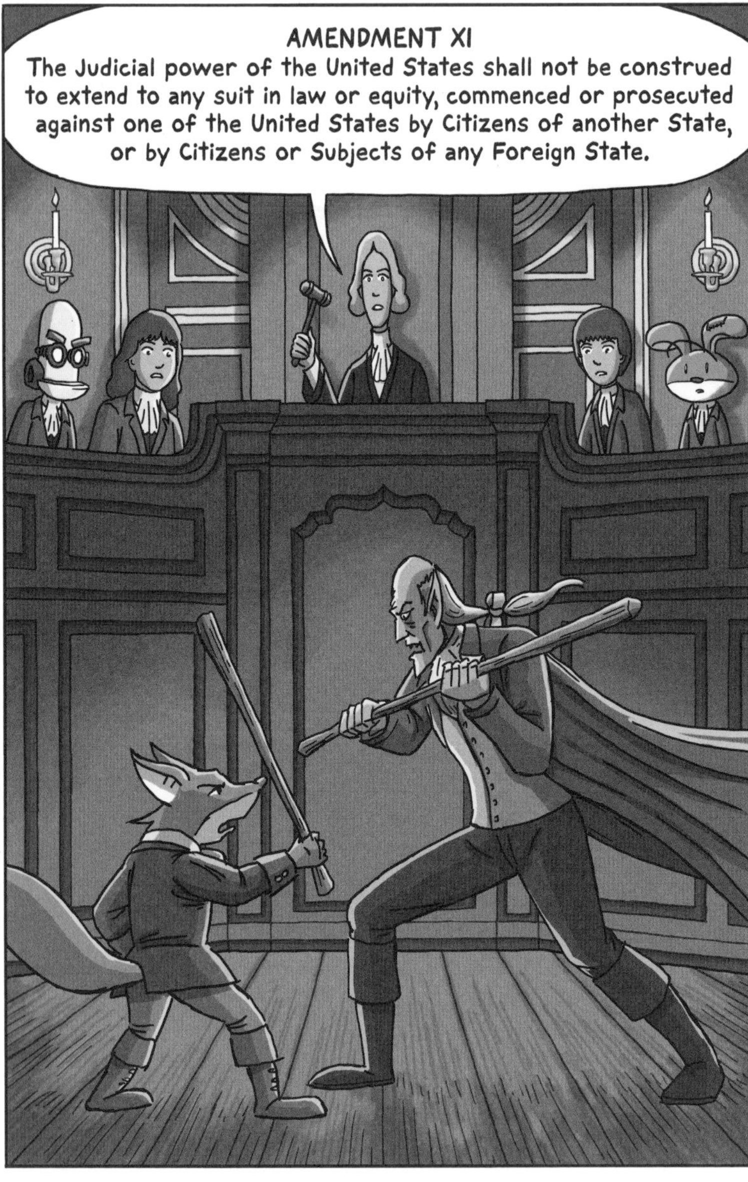
AMENDMENT XI
The Judicial power of the United States shall not be construed to extend to any suit in law or equity, commenced or prosecuted against one of the United States by Citizens of another State, or by Citizens or Subjects of any Foreign State.

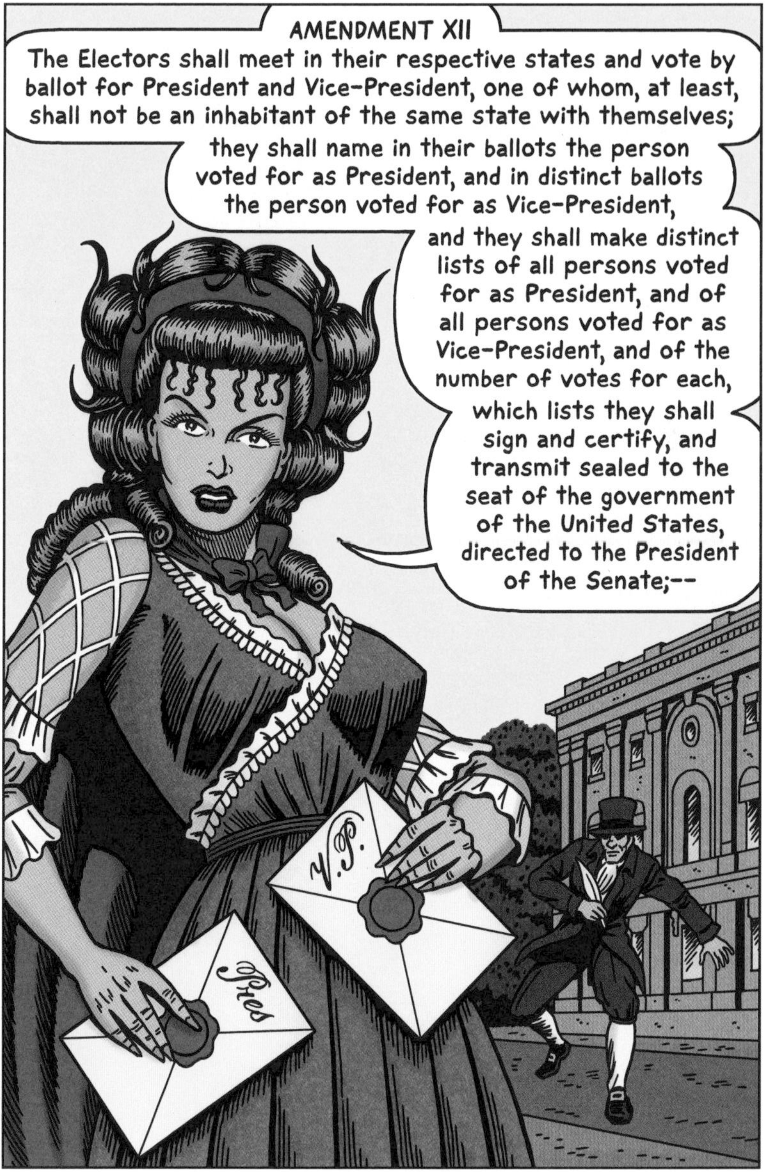
AMENDMENT XII
The Electors shall meet in their respective states and vote by ballot for President and Vice-President, one of whom, at least, shall not be an inhabitant of the same state with themselves;
they shall name in their ballots the person voted for as President, and in distinct ballots the person voted for as Vice-President,
and they shall make distinct lists of all persons voted for as President, and of all persons voted for as Vice-President, and of the number of votes for each,
which lists they shall sign and certify, and transmit sealed to the seat of the government of the United States, directed to the President of the Senate;--
V.P.
Pres

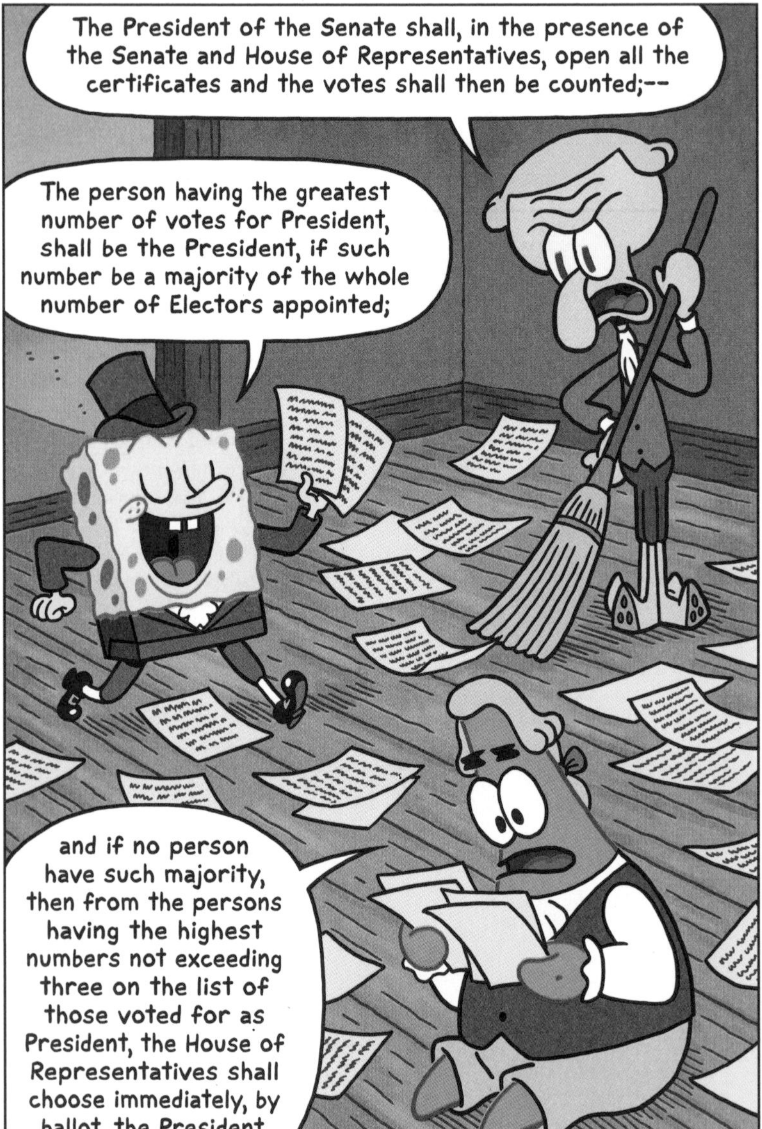
The President of the Senate shall, in the presence of the Senate and House of Representatives, open all the certificates and the votes shall then be counted;--
The person having the greatest number of votes for President, shall be the President, if such number be a majority of the whole number of Electors appointed;
and if no person have such majority, then from the persons having the highest numbers not exceeding three on the list of those voted for as President, the House of Representatives shall choose immediately, by ballot, the President.

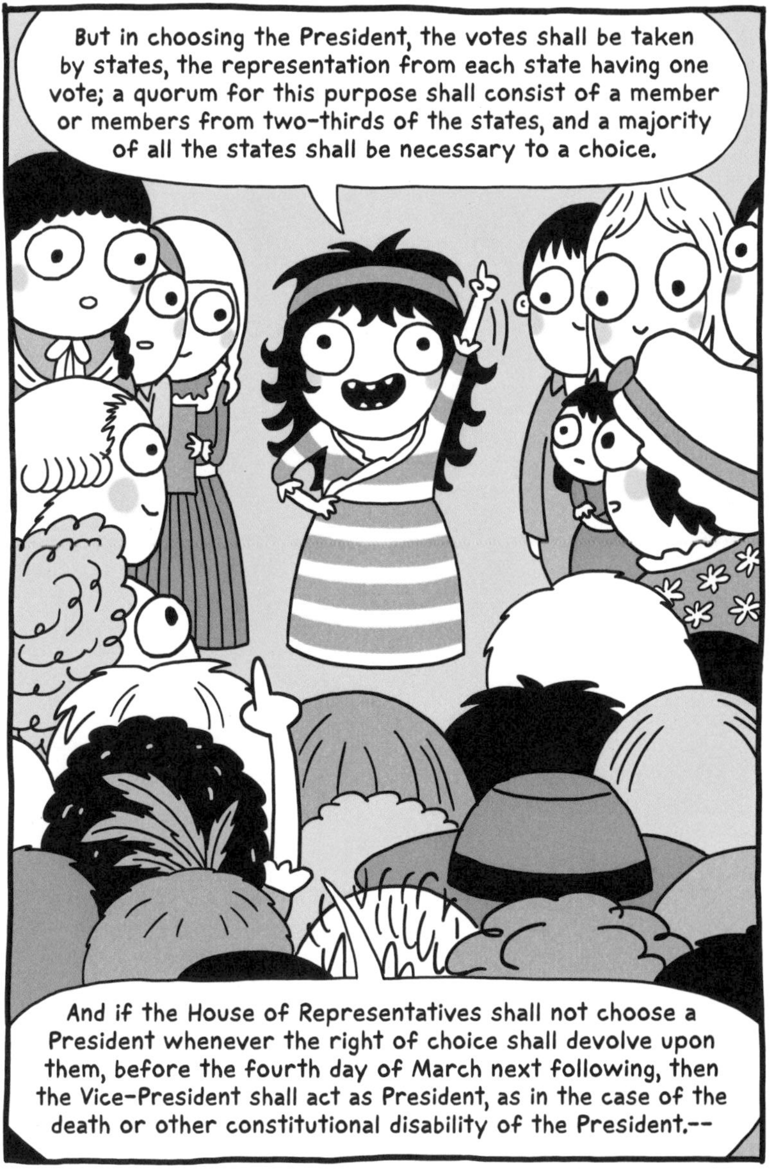

But in choosing the President, the votes shall be taken by states, the representation from each state having one vote; a quorum for this purpose shall consist of a member or members from two-thirds of the states, and a majority of all the states shall be necessary to a choice.
And if the House of Representatives shall not choose a President whenever the right of choice shall devolve upon them, before the fourth day of March next following, then the Vice-President shall act as President, as in the case of the death or other constitutional disability of the President.--

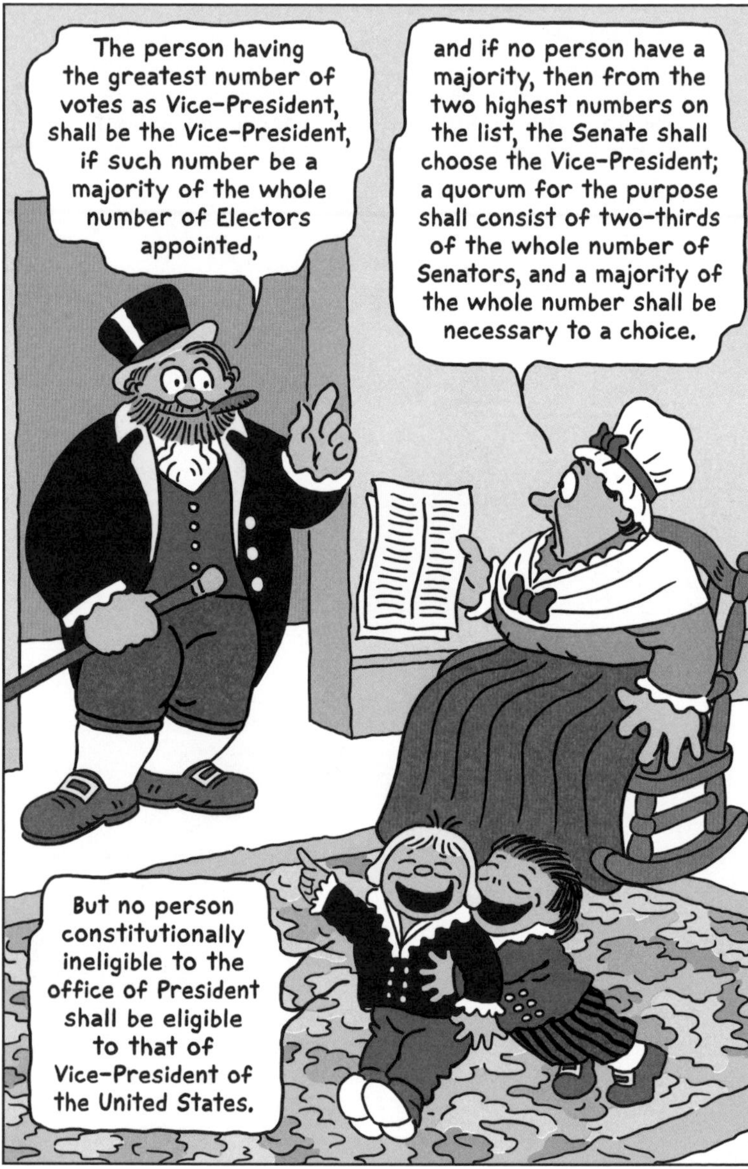
The person having the greatest number of votes as Vice-President, shall be the Vice-President, if such number be a majority of the whole number of Electors appointed,
and if no person have a majority, then from the two highest numbers on the list, the Senate shall choose the Vice-President; a quorum for the purpose shall consist of two-thirds of the whole number of Senators, and a majority of the whole number shall be necessary to a choice.
But no person constitutionally ineligible to the office of President shall be eligible to that of Vice-President of the United States.

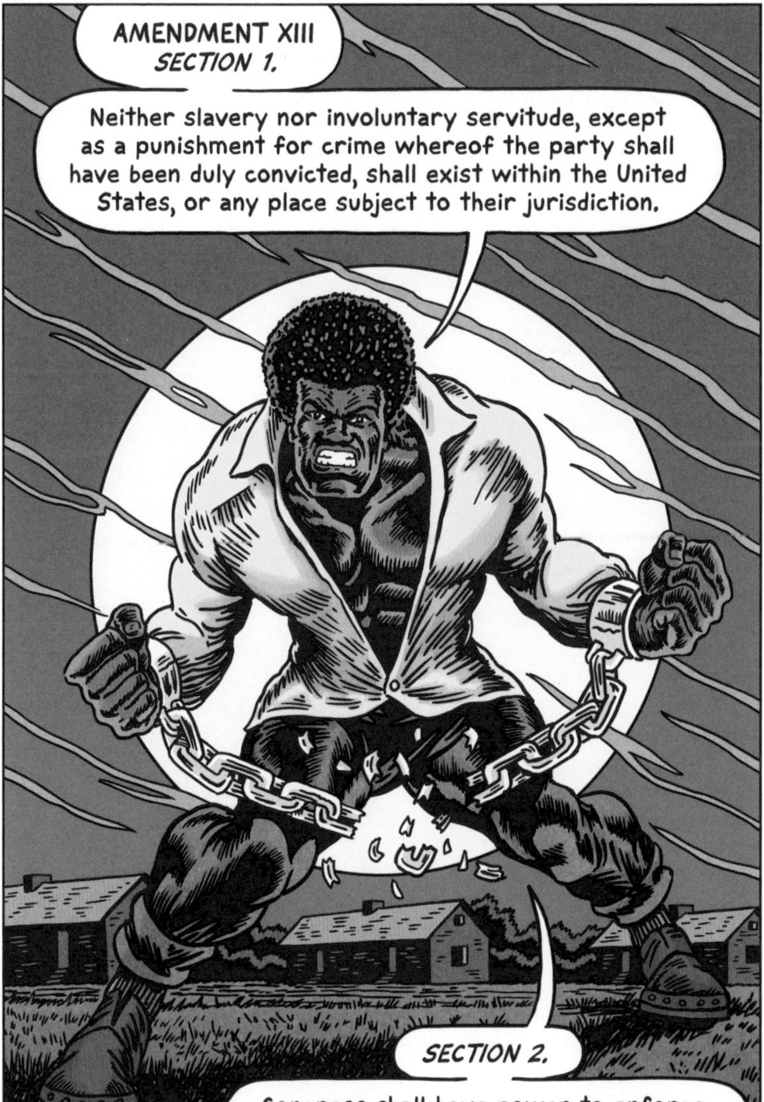
AMENDMENT XIII
SECTION 1.
Neither slavery nor involuntary servitude, except as a punishment for crime whereof the party shall have been duly convicted, shall exist within the United States, or any place subject to their jurisdiction.
SECTION 2.
Congress shall have power to enforce this article by appropriate legislation.

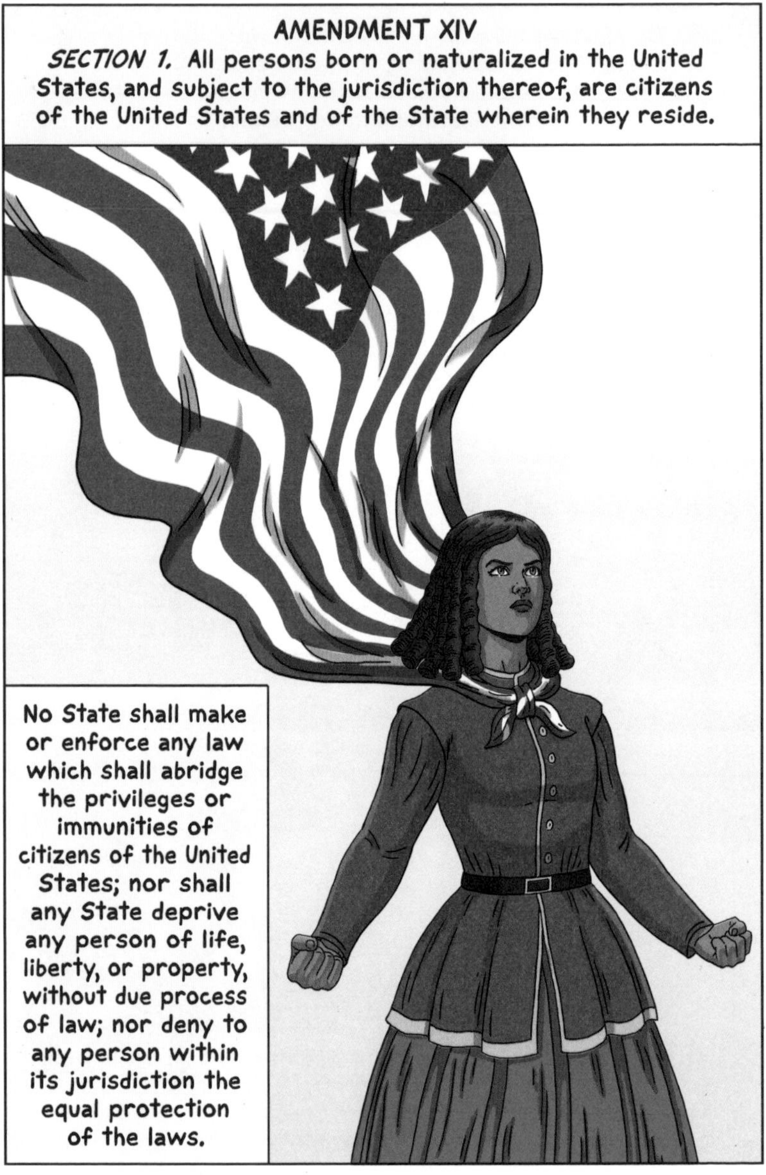
AMENDMENT XIV
SECTION 1. All persons born or naturalized in the United States, and subject to the jurisdiction thereof, are citizens of the United States and of the State wherein they reside.
No State shall make or enforce any law which shall abridge the privileges or immunities of citizens of the United States; nor shall any State deprive any person of life, liberty, or property, without due process of law; nor deny to any person within its jurisdiction the equal protection of the laws.

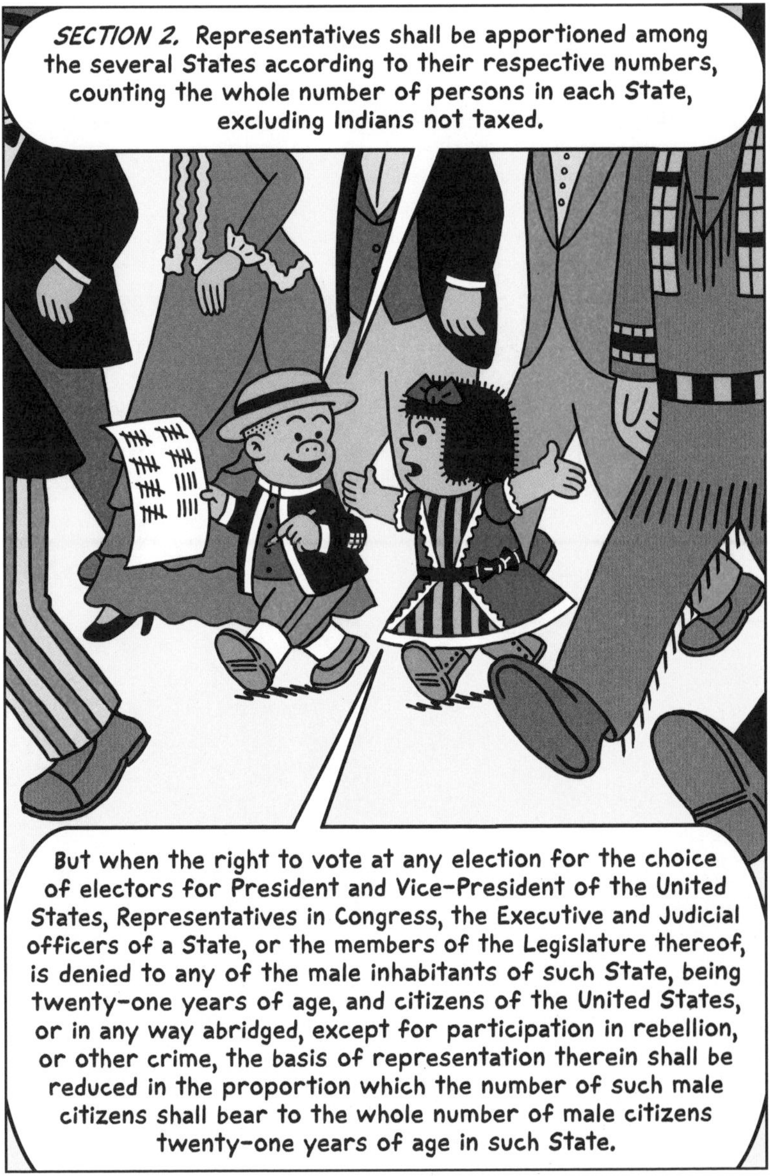
SECTION 2. Representatives shall be apportioned among the several States according to their respective numbers, counting the whole number of persons in each State, excluding Indians not taxed.
But when the right to vote at any election for the choice of electors for President and Vice-President of the United States, Representatives in Congress, the Executive and Judicial officers of a State, or the members of the Legislature thereof, is denied to any of the male inhabitants of such State, being twenty-one years of age, and citizens of the United States, or in any way abridged, except for participation in rebellion, or other crime, the basis of representation therein shall be reduced in the proportion which the number of such male citizens shall bear to the whole number of male citizens twenty-one years of age in such State.

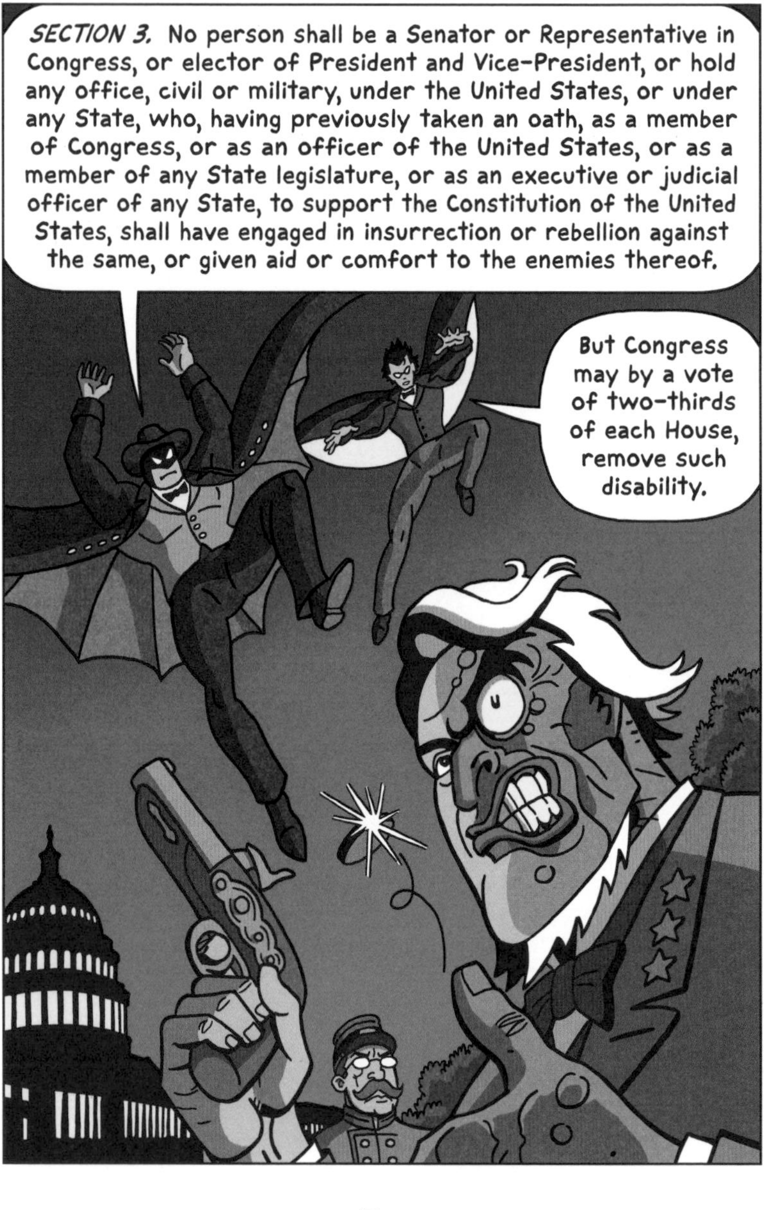
SECTION 3. No person shall be a Senator or Representative in Congress, or elector of President and Vice-President, or hold any office, civil or military, under the United States, or under any State, who, having previously taken an oath, as a member of Congress, or as an officer of the United States, or as a member of any State legislature, or as an executive or judicial officer of any State, to support the Constitution of the United States, shall have engaged in insurrection or rebellion against the same, or given aid or comfort to the enemies thereof.
But Congress may by a vote of two-thirds of each House, remove such disability.

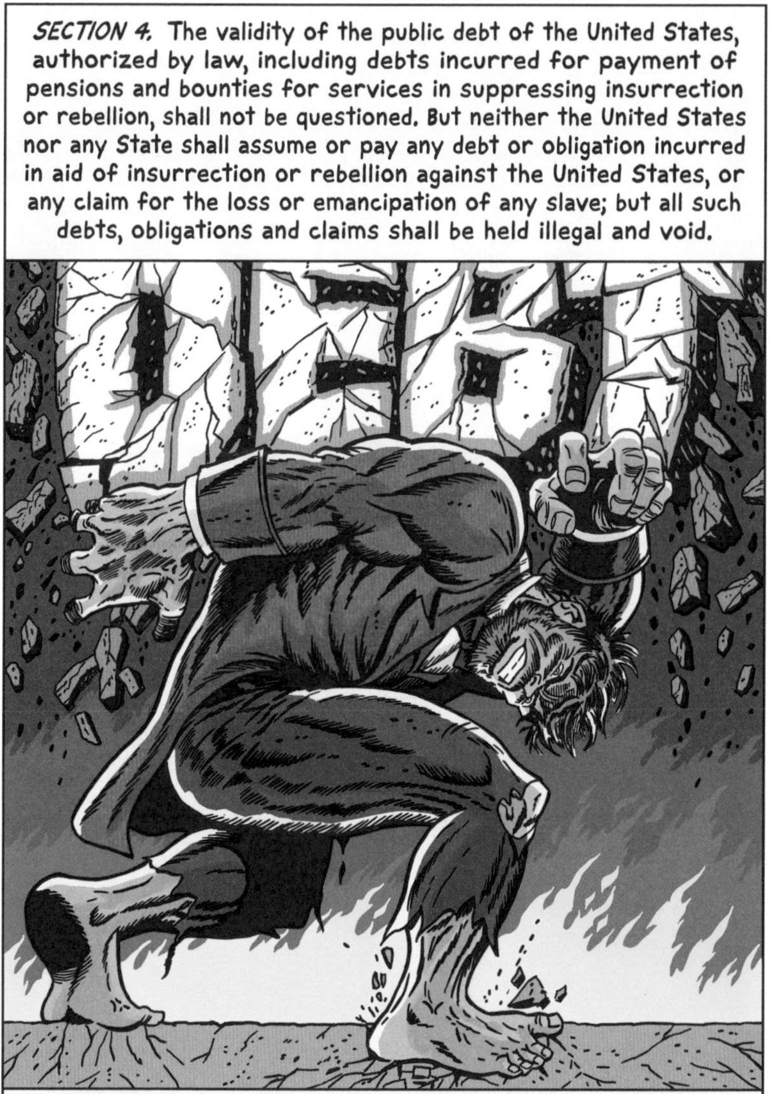
SECTION 4. The validity of the public debt of the United States, authorized by law, including debts incurred for payment of pensions and bounties for services in suppressing insurrection or rebellion, shall not be questioned. But neither the United States nor any State shall assume or pay any debt or obligation incurred in aid of insurrection or rebellion against the United States, or any claim for the loss or emancipation of any slave; but all such debts, obligations and claims shall be held illegal and void.
SECTION 5. The Congress shall have power to enforce, by appropriate legislation, the provisions of this article.

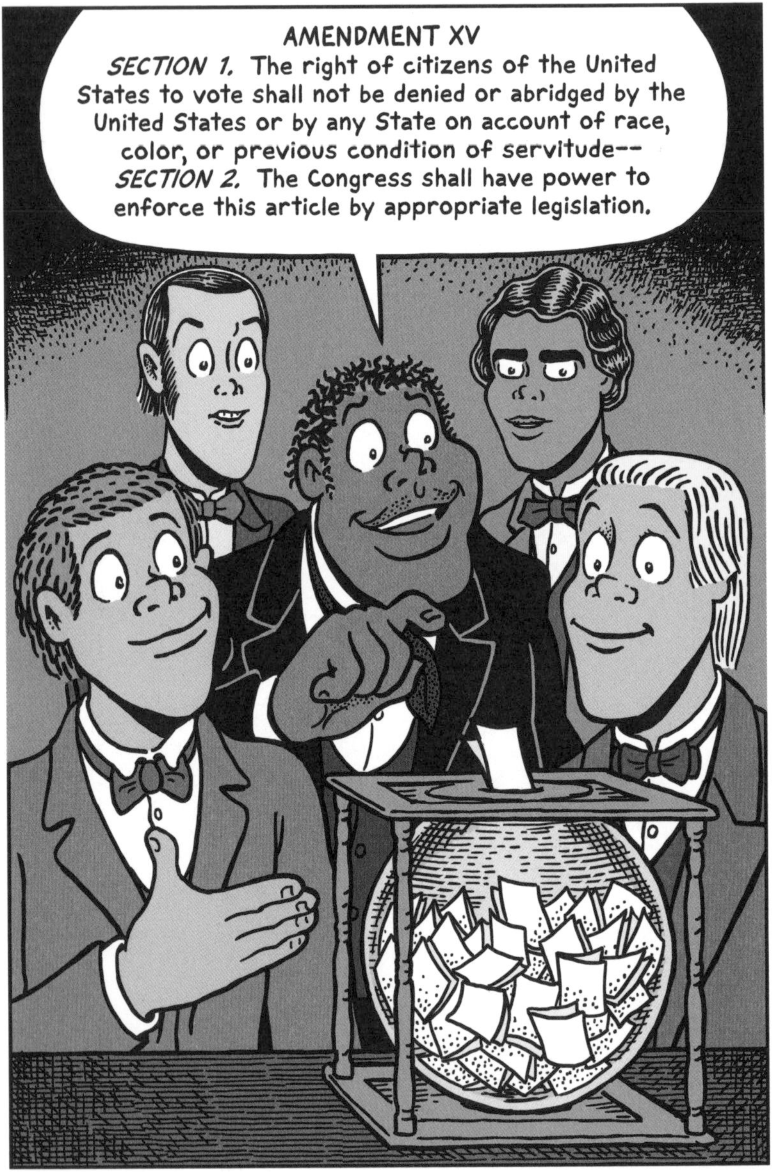
AMENDMENT XV
SECTION 1. The right of citizens of the United States to vote shall not be denied or abridged by the United States or by any State on account of race, color, or previous condition of servitude-- SECTION 2. The Congress shall have power to enforce this article by appropriate legislation.

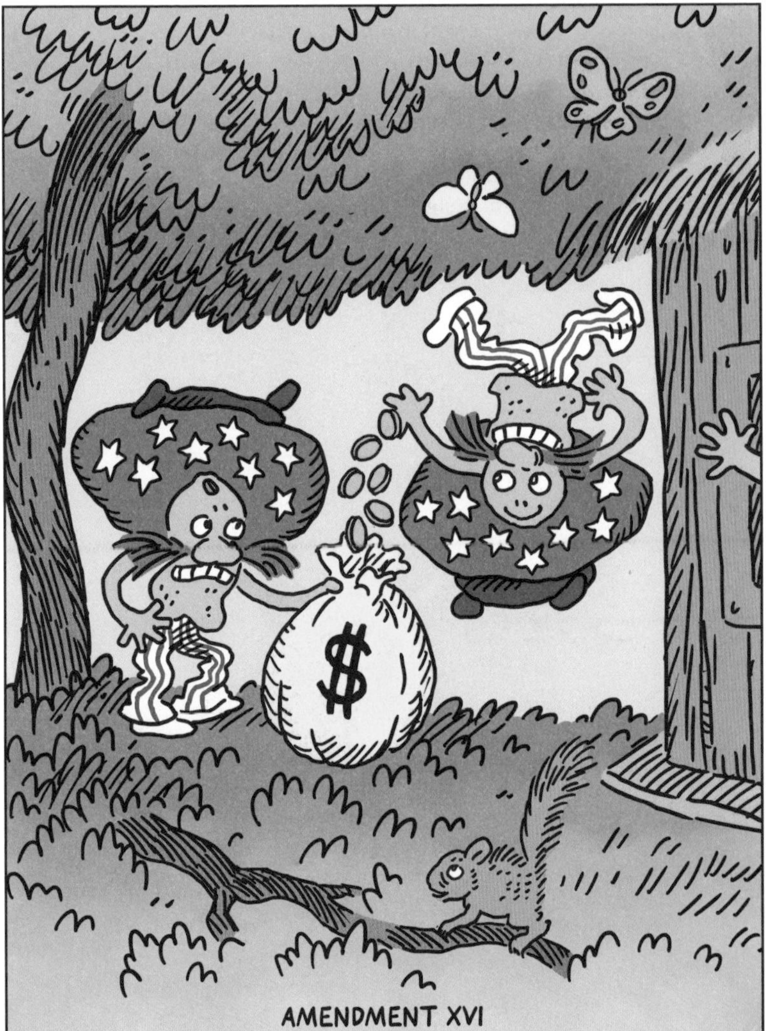

AMENDMENT XVI

The Congress shall have power to lay and collect taxes on incomes, from whatever source derived, without apportionment among the several States, and without regard to any census or enumeration.

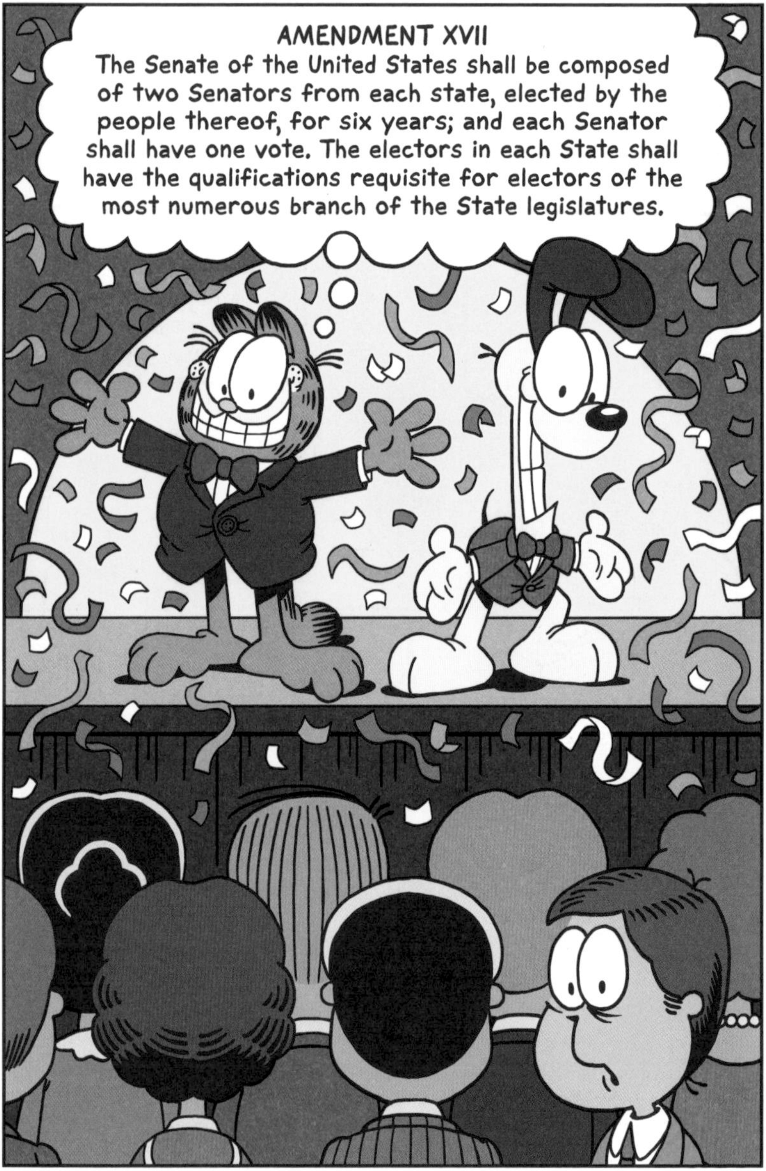
AMENDMENT XVII
The Senate of the United States shall be composed of two Senators from each state, elected by the people thereof, for six years; and each Senator shall have one vote. The electors in each State shall have the qualifications requisite for electors of the most numerous branch of the State legislatures.

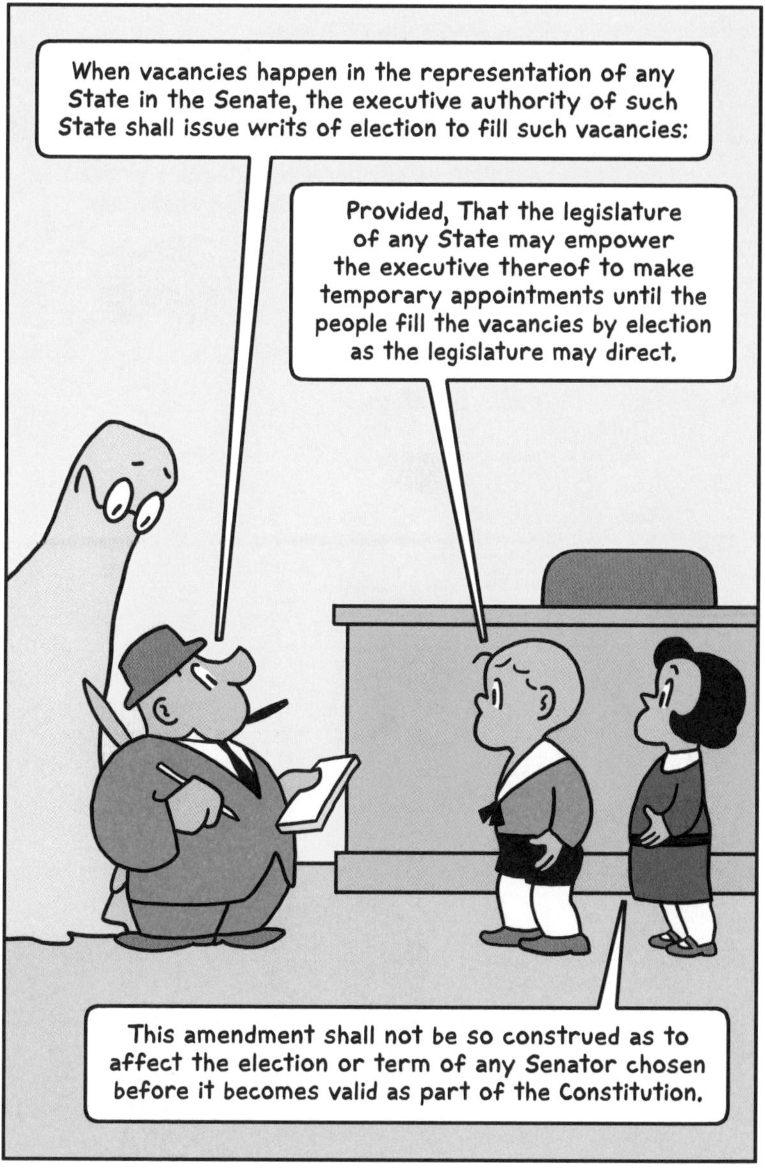

When vacancies happen in the representation of any State in the Senate, the executive authority of such State shall issue writs of election to fill such vacancies:
Provided, That the legislature of any State may empower the executive thereof to make temporary appointments until the people fill the vacancies by election as the legislature may direct.
This amendment shall not be so construed as to affect the election or term of any Senator chosen before it becomes valid as part of the Constitution.

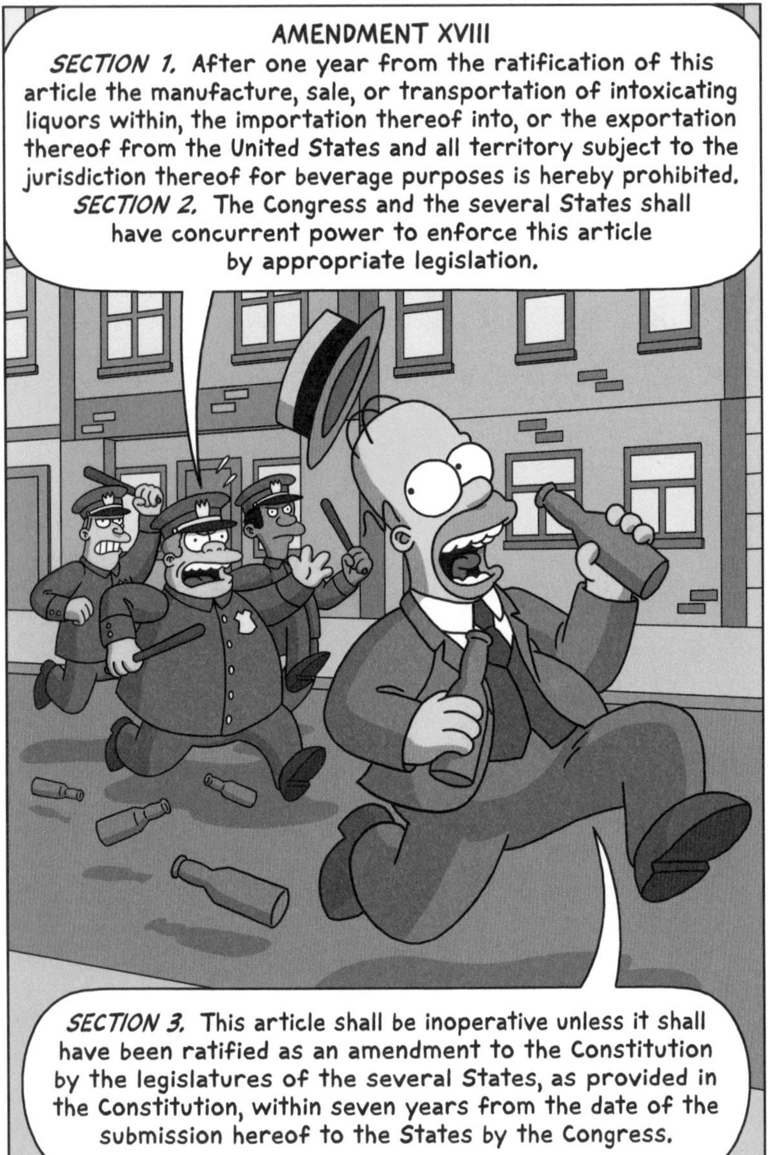

AMENDMENT XVIII
SECTION 1. After one year from the ratification of this article the manufacture, sale, or transportation of intoxicating liquors within, the importation thereof into, or the exportation thereof from the United States and all territory subject to the jurisdiction thereof for beverage purposes is hereby prohibited.
SECTION 2. The Congress and the several States shall have concurrent power to enforce this article by appropriate legislation.
SECTION 3. This article shall be inoperative unless it shall have been ratified as an amendment to the Constitution by the legislatures of the several States, as provided in the Constitution, within seven years from the date of the submission hereof to the States by the Congress.

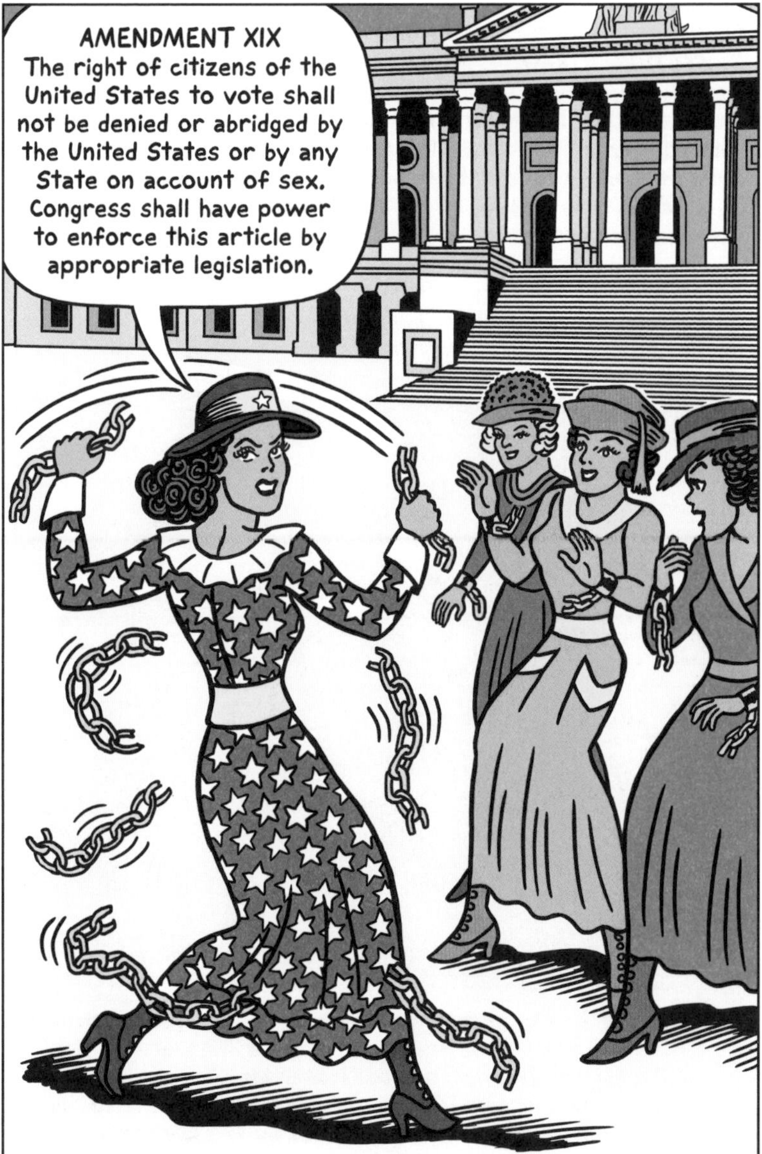
AMENDMENT XIX
The right of citizens of the United States to vote shall not be denied or abridged by the United States or by any State on account of sex. Congress shall have power to enforce this article by appropriate legislation.

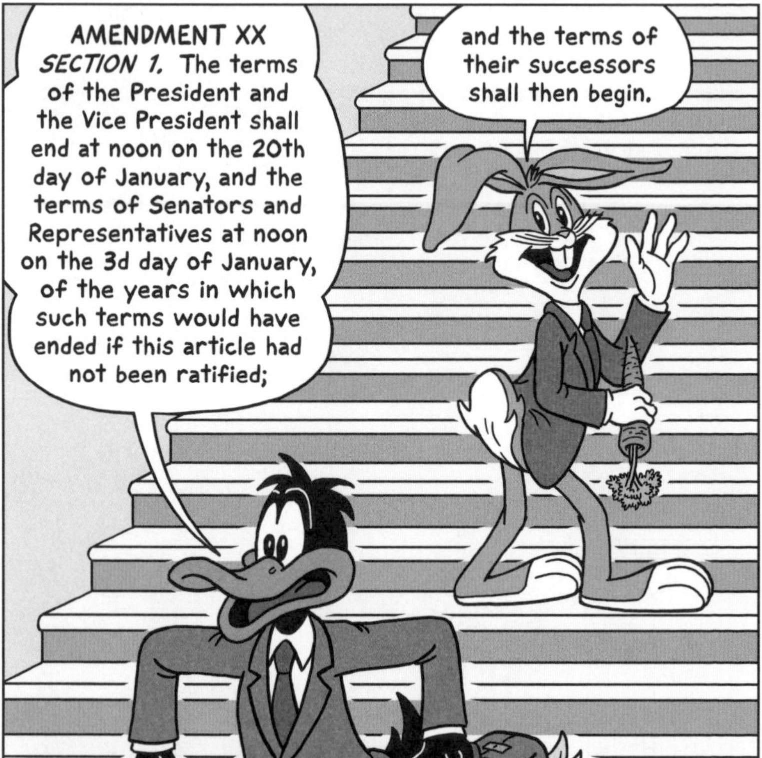
AMENDMENT XX SECTION 1. The terms of the President and the Vice President shall end at noon on the 20th day of January, and the terms of Senators and Representatives at noon on the 3d day of January, of the years in which such terms would have ended if this article had not been ratified;
and the terms of their successors shall then begin.
SECTION 2. The Congress shall assemble at least once in every year, and such meeting shall begin at noon on the 3d day of January, unless they shall by law appoint a different day.

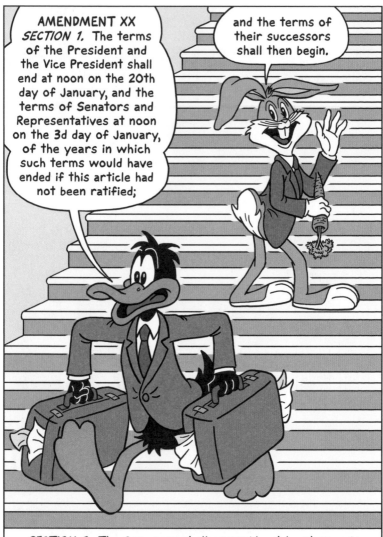

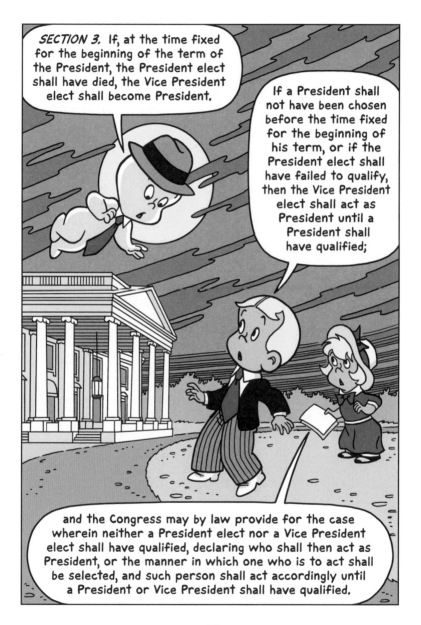

SECTION 3. If, at the time fixed for the beginning of the term of the President, the President elect shall have died, the Vice President elect shall become President.

If a President shall not have been chosen before the time fixed for the beginning of his term, or if the President elect shall have failed to qualify, then the Vice President elect shall act as President until a President shall have qualified;

and the Congress may by law provide for the case wherein neither a President elect nor a Vice President elect shall have qualified, declaring who shall then act as President, or the manner in which one who is to act shall be selected, and such person shall act accordingly until a President or Vice President shall have qualified.

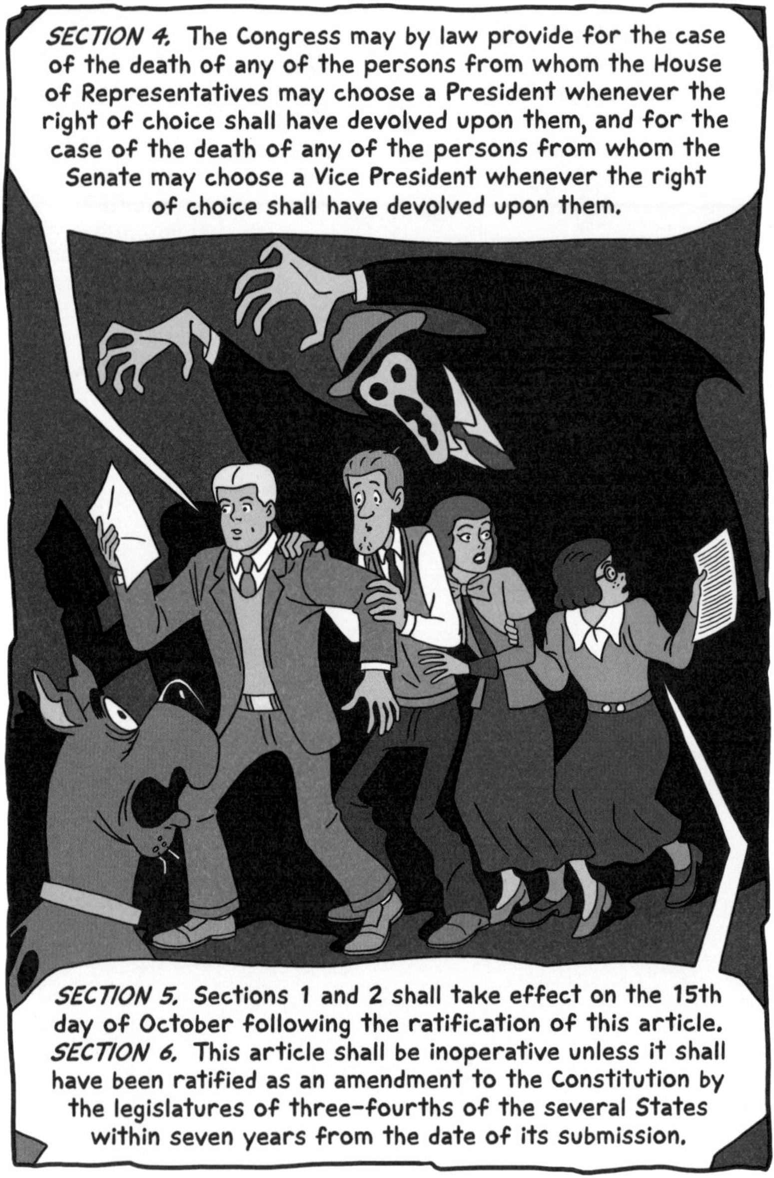
SECTION 4. The Congress may by law provide for the case of the death of any of the persons from whom the House of Representatives may choose a President whenever the right of choice shall have devolved upon them, and for the case of the death of any of the persons from whom the Senate may choose a Vice President whenever the right of choice shall have devolved upon them.
SECTION 5. Sections 1 and 2 shall take effect on the 15th day of October following the ratification of this article.
SECTION 6. This article shall be inoperative unless it shall have been ratified as an amendment to the Constitution by the legislatures of three-fourths of the several States within seven years from the date of its submission.

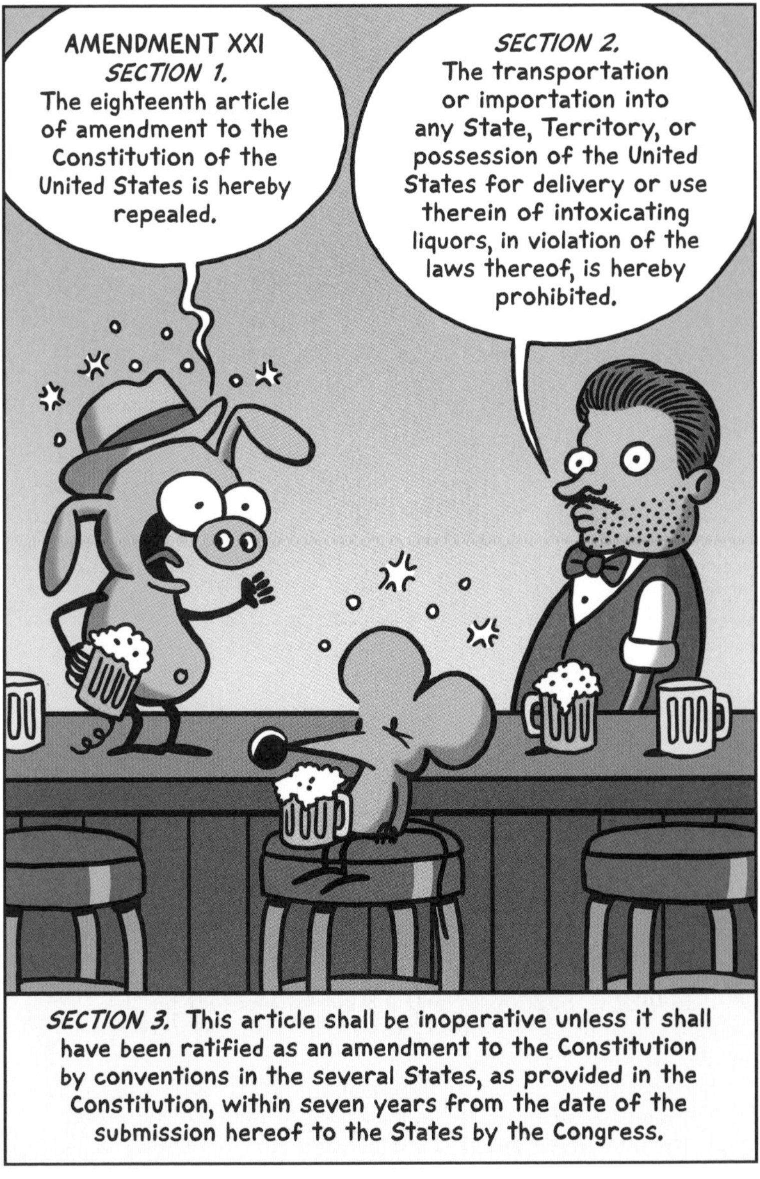
AMENDMENT XXI
SECTION 1.
The eighteenth article of amendment to the Constitution of the United States is hereby repealed.
SECTION 2.
The transportation or importation into any State, Territory, or possession of the United States for delivery or use therein of intoxicating liquors, in violation of the laws thereof, is hereby prohibited.
SECTION 3. This article shall be inoperative unless it shall have been ratified as an amendment to the Constitution by conventions in the several States, as provided in the Constitution, within seven years from the date of the submission hereof to the States by the Congress.

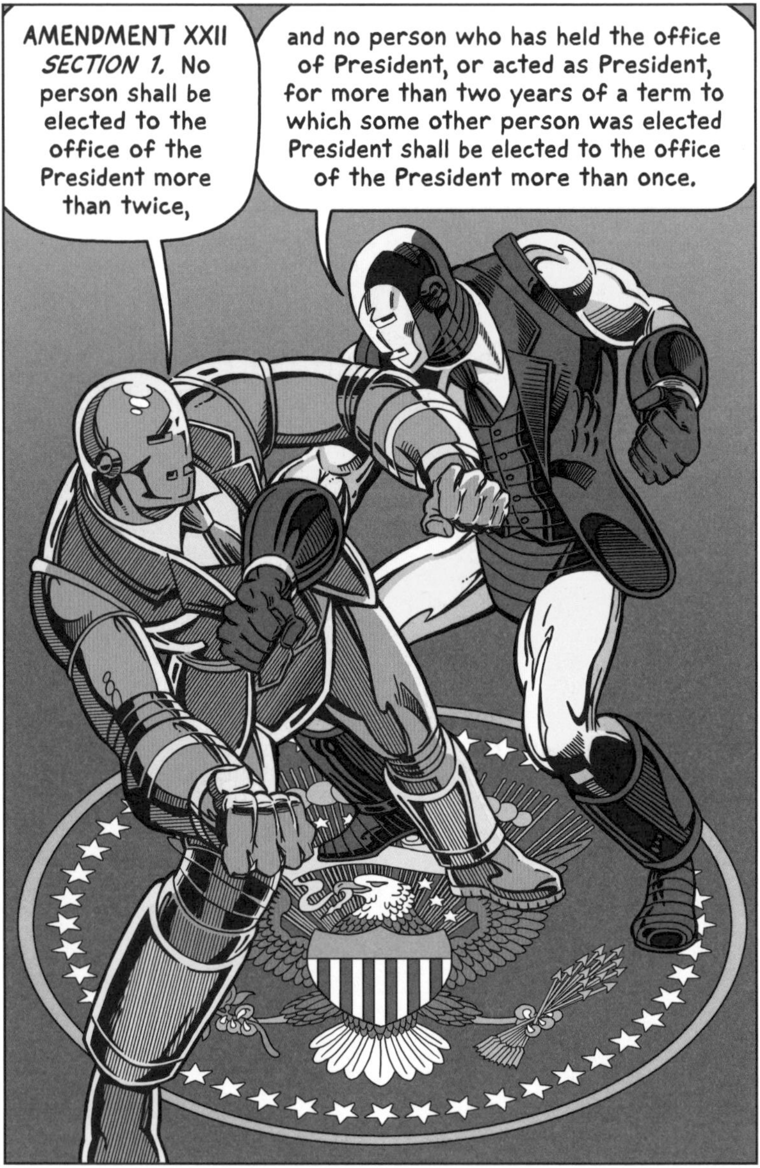
AMENDMENT XXII *SECTION 1.* No person shall be elected to the office of the President more than twice,
and no person who has held the office of President, or acted as President, for more than two years of a term to which some other person was elected President shall be elected to the office of the President more than once.

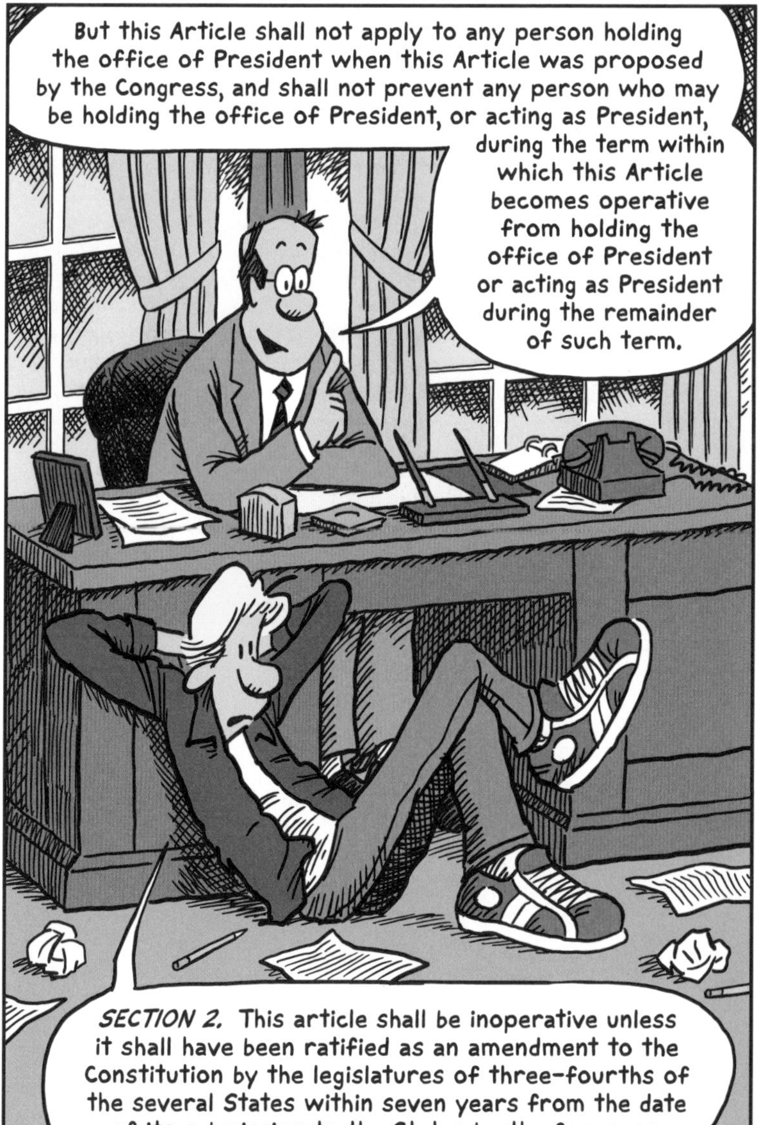
But this Article shall not apply to any person holding the office of President when this Article was proposed by the Congress, and shall not prevent any person who may be holding the office of President, or acting as President, during the term within which this Article becomes operative from holding the office of President or acting as President during the remainder of such term.
SECTION 2. This article shall be inoperative unless it shall have been ratified as an amendment to the Constitution by the legislatures of three-fourths of the several States within seven years from the date of its submission to the States by the Congress.

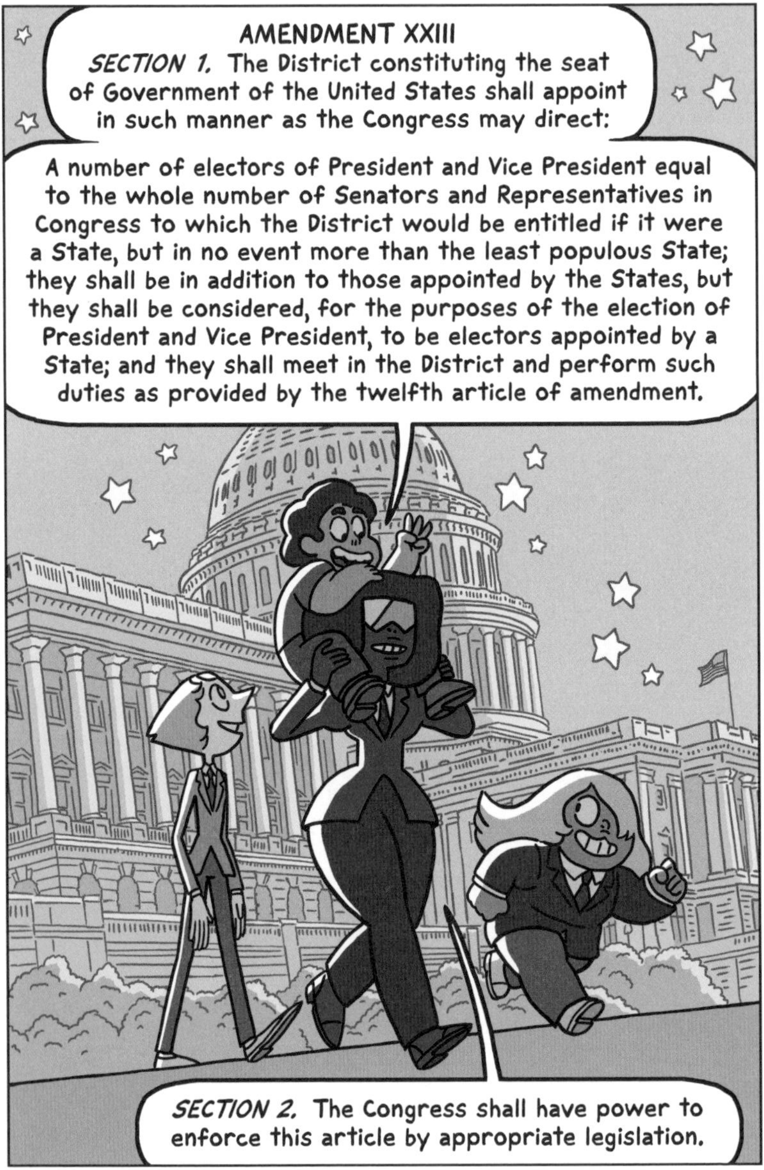
AMENDMENT XXIII
SECTION 1. The District constituting the seat of Government of the United States shall appoint in such manner as the Congress may direct:
A number of electors of President and Vice President equal to the whole number of Senators and Representatives in Congress to which the District would be entitled if it were a State, but in no event more than the least populous State; they shall be in addition to those appointed by the States, but they shall be considered, for the purposes of the election of President and Vice President, to be electors appointed by a State; and they shall meet in the District and perform such duties as provided by the twelfth article of amendment.
SECTION 2. The Congress shall have power to enforce this article by appropriate legislation.

AMENDMENT XXIV

SECTION 1. The right of citizens of the United States to vote in any primary or other election for President or Vice President, for electors for President or Vice President, or for Senator or Representative in Congress, shall not be denied or abridged by the United States or any State by reason of failure to pay any poll tax or other tax.

SECTION 2. The Congress shall have power to enforce this article by appropriate legislation.

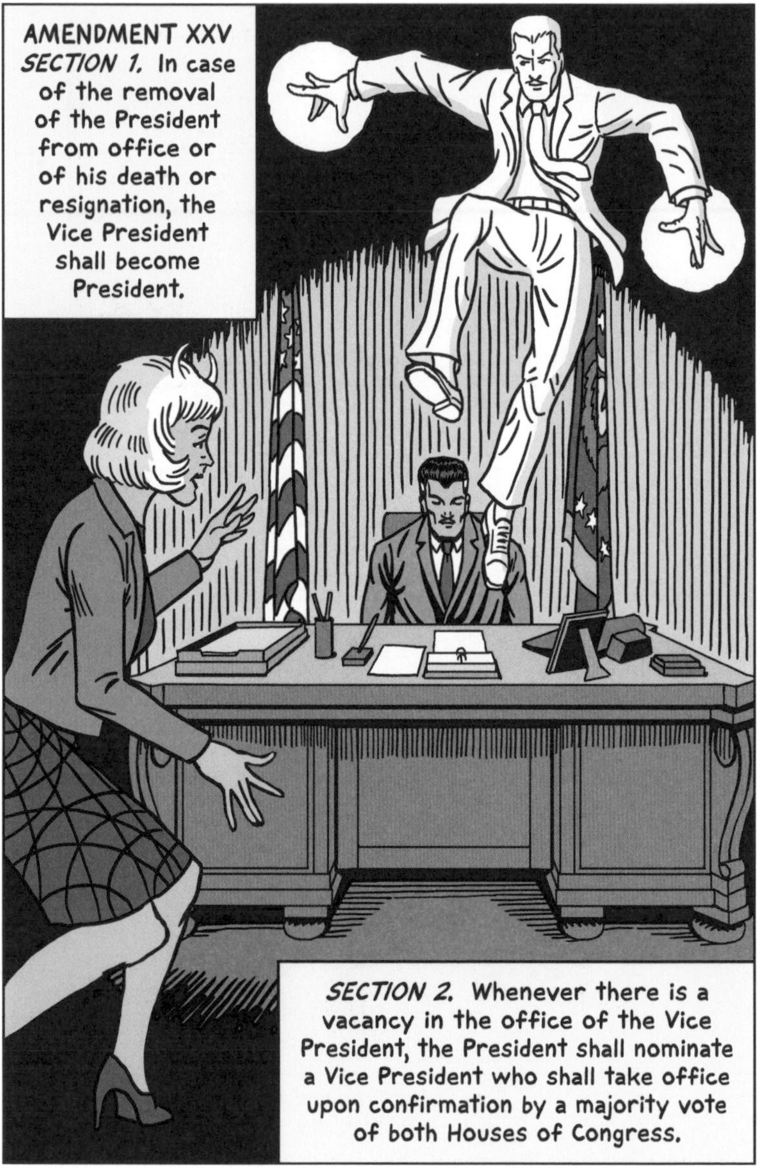
AMENDMENT XXV
SECTION 1. In case of the removal of the President from office or of his death or resignation, the Vice President shall become President.
SECTION 2. Whenever there is a vacancy in the office of the Vice President, the President shall nominate a Vice President who shall take office upon confirmation by a majority vote of both Houses of Congress.

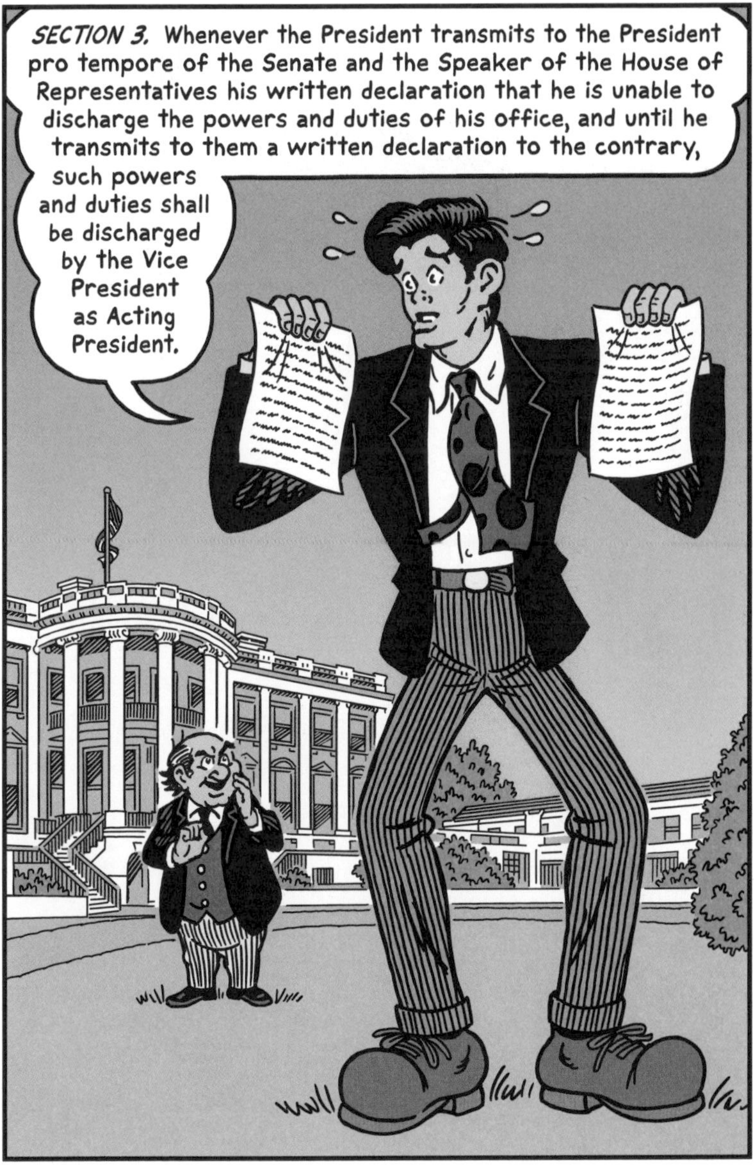
SECTION 3. Whenever the President transmits to the President pro tempore of the Senate and the Speaker of the House of Representatives his written declaration that he is unable to discharge the powers and duties of his office, and until he transmits to them a written declaration to the contrary,
such powers and duties shall be discharged by the Vice President as Acting President.

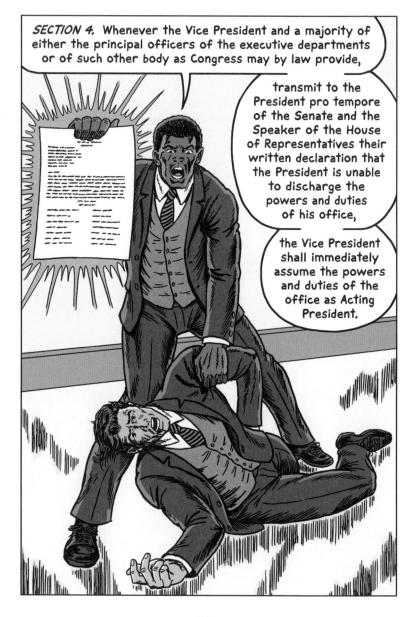

SECTION 4. Whenever the Vice President and a majority of either the principal officers of the executive departments or of such other body as Congress may by law provide,

transmit to the President pro tempore of the Senate and the Speaker of the House of Representatives their written declaration that the President is unable to discharge the powers and duties of his office,

the Vice President shall immediately assume the powers and duties of the office as Acting President.

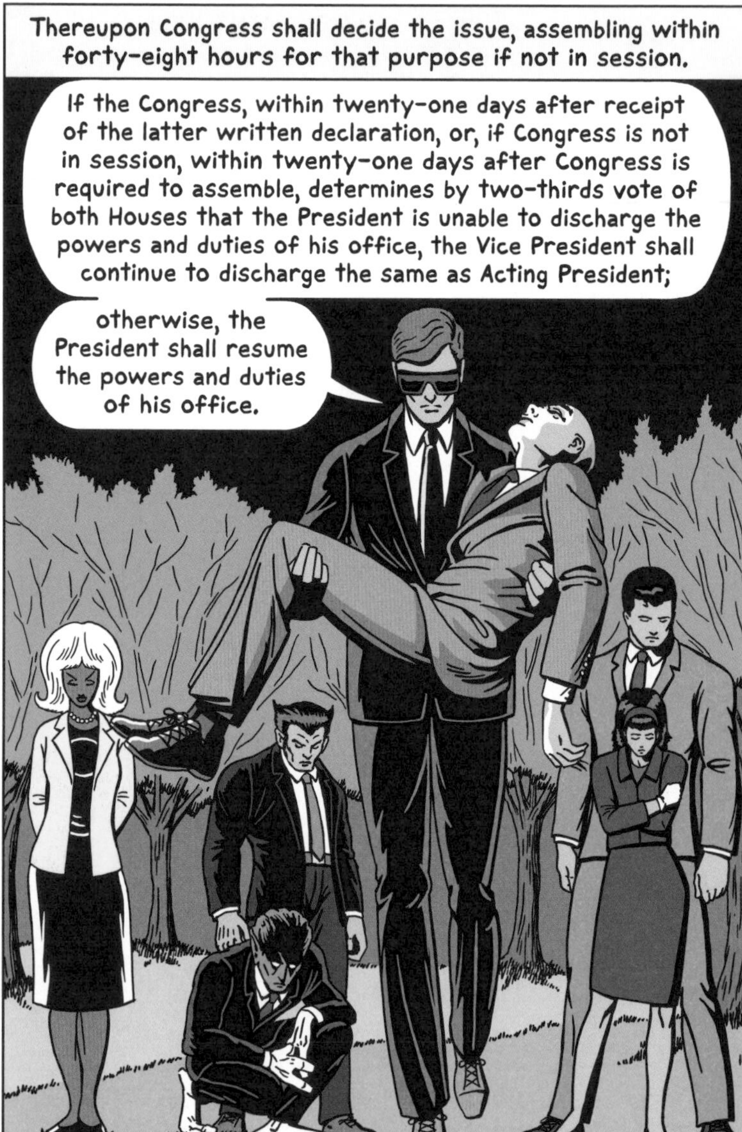
Thereupon Congress shall decide the issue, assembling within forty-eight hours for that purpose if not in session.
If the Congress, within twenty-one days after receipt of the latter written declaration, or, if Congress is not in session, within twenty-one days after Congress is required to assemble, determines by two-thirds vote of both Houses that the President is unable to discharge the powers and duties of his office, the Vice President shall continue to discharge the same as Acting President;
otherwise, the President shall resume the powers and duties of his office.

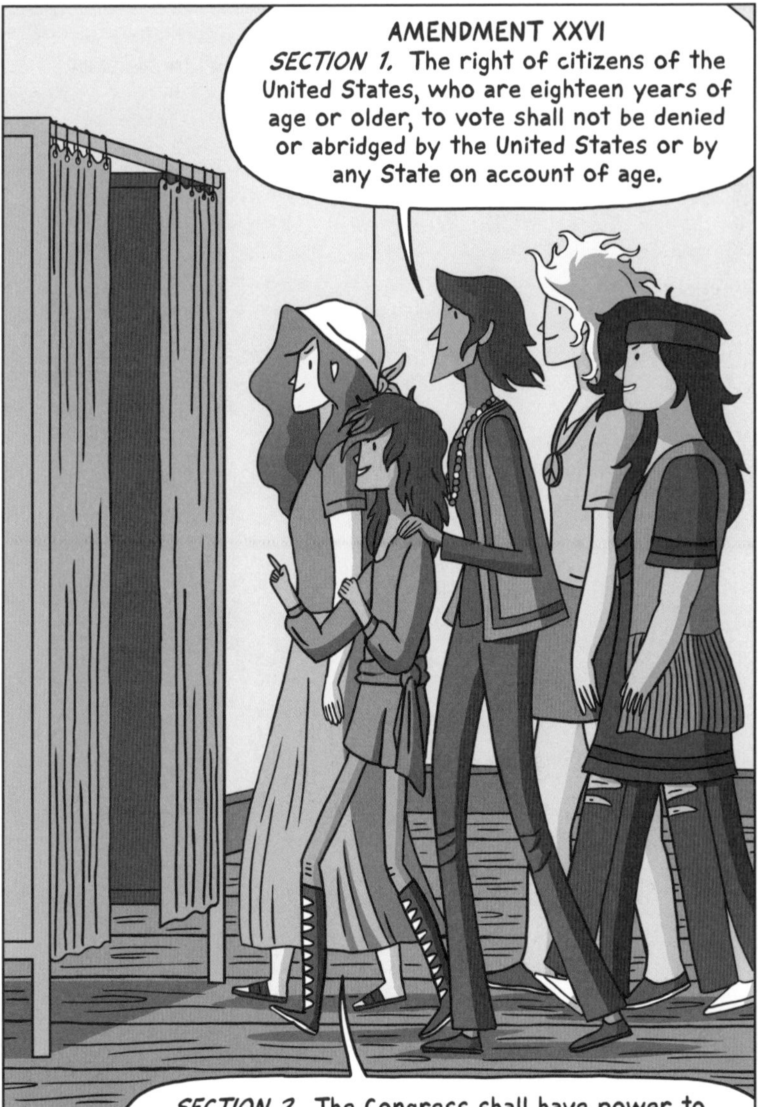
AMENDMENT XXVI
SECTION 1. The right of citizens of the United States, who are eighteen years of age or older, to vote shall not be denied or abridged by the United States or by any State on account of age.
SECTION 2. The Congress shall have power to enforce this article by appropriate legislation.

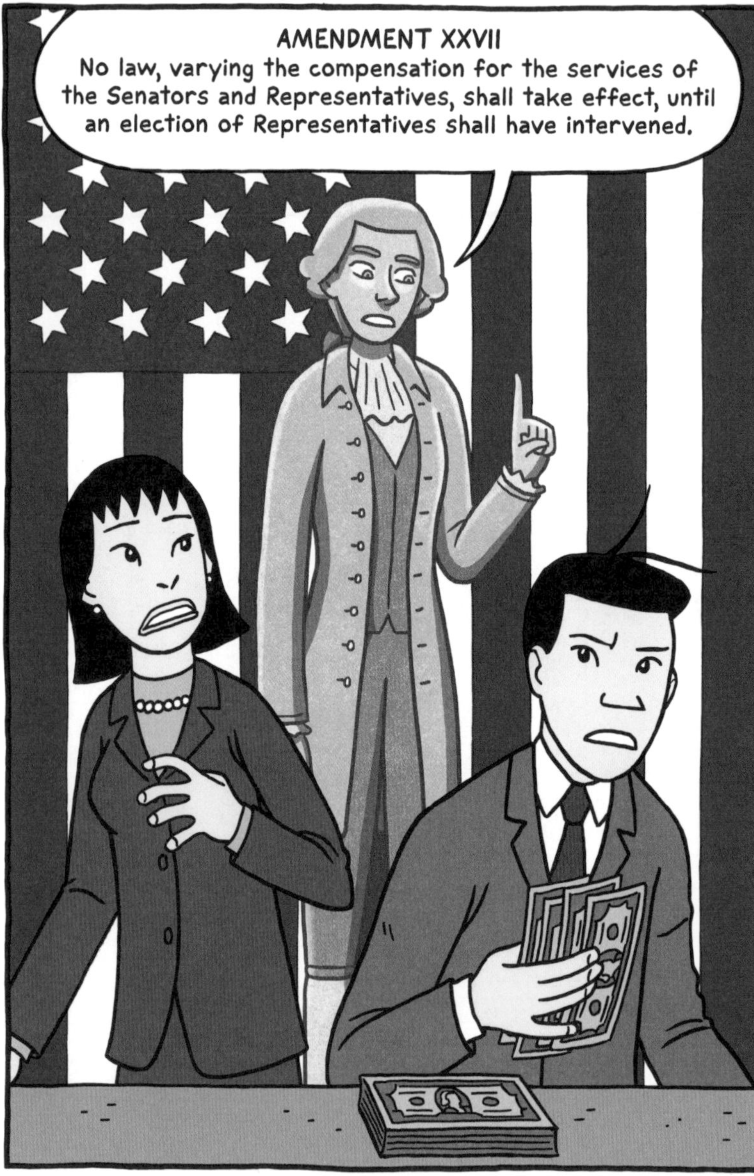
AMENDMENT XXVII
No law, varying the compensation for the services of the Senators and Representatives, shall take effect, until an election of Representatives shall have intervened.

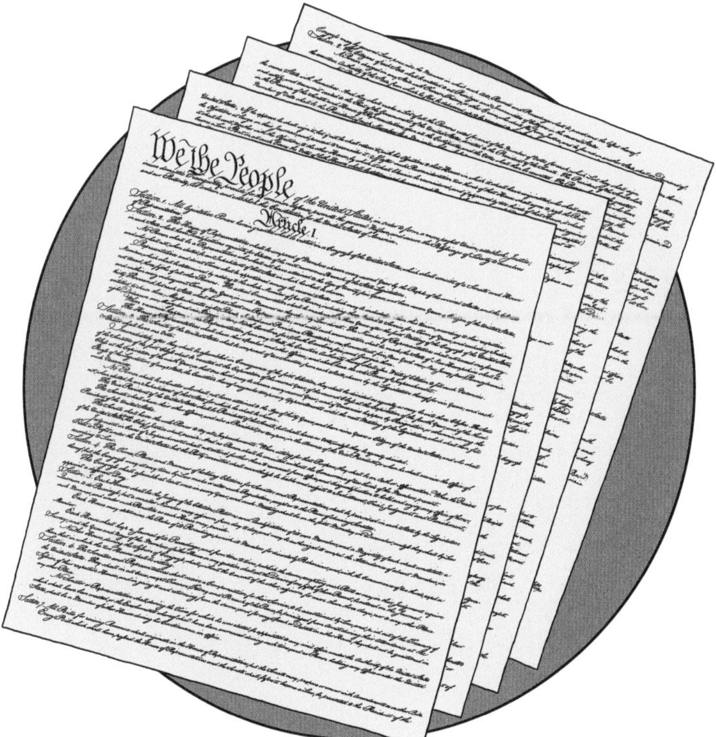
We the People
Article. I

Comics Index

These are the original comics sources used as inspiration for each page.

Page 5: Alex Raymond, *Flash Gordon*, c. 1935.

Page 6: Raina Telgemeier, *Sisters*, *Drama*, and *Ghosts*, c. 2016.

Page 7: José Luis García-López and Bob Oksner, *Superman* and *The Flash*, 1976.

Page 8: Hank Ketcham, *Dennis the Menace*, c. 1975.

Page 9: Phil Davis, *Mandrake*, 1946.

Page 10: Bill Amend, *Foxtrot*, c. 2003.

Page 11: Hilda Terry, *Teena*, 1954.

Page 12: Bud Fisher, *Mutt and Jeff*, c. 1928.

Page 13: Grace G. Drayton, *Dolly Dimples*, 1914.

Page 14: Mike Mignola, *Hellboy*, c. 1999.

Page 15: John Romita Sr., *The Amazing Spider-Man*, 1969.

Page 16: Alison Bechdel, *Dykes to Watch Out For*, c. 2004.

Page 17: Chris Houghton, *Adventure Time*, 2013.

Page 18: Frederick Burr Opper, *Happy Hooligan*, 1910.

Page 19: Nicole Hollander, *Sylvia*, 1990.

Page 20: Harold Gray, *Little Orphan Annie*, 1940.

Page 21: Gladys Parker, *Mopsy*, 1955.

Page 22: Ramona Fradon and Bob Smith, *Super Friends*, 1980.

Page 23: Patrick McDonnell, *Mutts*, 2000.

Page 24: Jeff Kinney, *Diary of a Wimpy Kid*, c. 2008.

Page 25: Marie Severin, *Muppet Babies*, 1987.

Page 26: Carl Barks, *Uncle Scrooge*, c. 1956.

Page 27: Chic Young, *Blondie*, c. 1955.

Page 28: Joe Kubert, *Sgt. Rock*, 1981.

Page 29: Mort Walker, *Beetle Bailey*, c. 1980.

Page 30: Frank King, *Gasoline Alley*, c. 1929.

Page 31: George Herriman, *Krazy Kat*, c. 1936.

Page 32: CJ Cannon, *Rick and Morty*, 2015.

Page 33: E. C. Segar, *Thimble Theatre Starring Popeye*, 1933.

Page 34: Cathy Guisewite, *Cathy*, 2008.

Page 35: Hal Foster, *Prince Valiant*, c. 1940.

Page 36: Amanda Conner and Jeff Albrecht, *Barbie*, 1993.

Page 37: Lynda Barry, *Marlys (Ernie Pook's Comeek)*, c. 1989.

Page 38: Alex Schomburg, *Captain America*, 1943.

Page 39: C. C. Beck, *Captain Marvel (The Marvel Family)*, 1945.

Page 40: Jaime and Gilbert Hernandez, *Love and Rockets*, 1996.

Page 41: Jeff Smith, *Bone*, 1993.

Page 42: Winsor McCay, *Little Nemo (In the Land of Wonderful Dreams)*, 1912.

Page 43: Garry Trudeau, *Doonesbury*, 1990.

Page 44: Fiona Staples, *Saga*, c. 2015.

Page 45: Jack Davis, *The Crypt Keeper (Tales From the Crypt)*, 1955.

Page 46: Bill Hoest, *The Lockhorns*, 1970.

Page 47: Ken Ernst, *Mary Worth*, 1967.

Page 48: Jim Lee and Scott Williams, *WildC.A.T.s*, 1992.

Page 49: Lyonel Feininger, *The Kin-der-Kids*, 1906.

Page 50: Tarpé Mills, *Miss Fury*, c. 1946.

Page 51: Dan and Jim DeCarlo, *Archie*, 1988.

Page 52: George McManus, *Bringing up Father*, 1945.

Page 53: Walter Simonson, *The Mighty Thor*, 1987.

Page 54: Gary Larson, *The Far Side*, c. 1989.

Page 55: Adrian Tomine, *Optic Nerve (Sleepwalk* and *Shortcomings)*, c. 2007.

Page 56: Bud Counihan, *Betty Boop*, 1935.

Page 57: Al Kilgore, *Bullwinkle*, c. 1962.

Page 58: Rose O'Neill, *The Kewpies*, c. 1936.

Page 59: Chester Gould, *Dick Tracy*, c. 1956.

Page 60: Dana Simpson, *Phoebe and Her Unicorn*, c. 2016.

Page 61: Gustavo "Gus" Arriola, *Gordo*, c. 1975.

Page 62: Joe Maneely, *Rawhide Kid*, 1957.

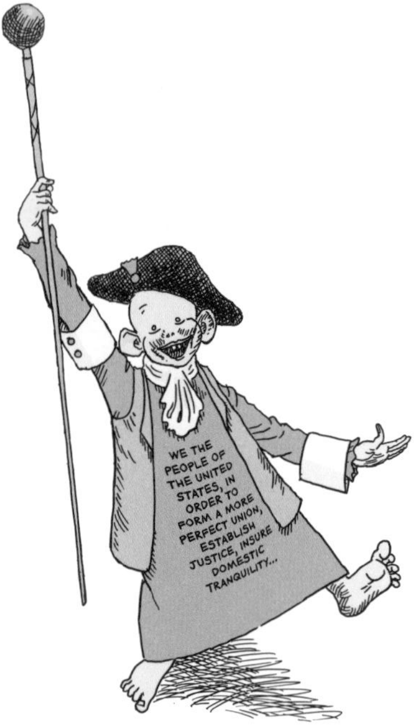
WE THE PEOPLE OF THE UNITED STATES, IN ORDER TO FORM A MORE PERFECT UNION, ESTABLISH JUSTICE, INSURE DOMESTIC TRANQUILITY...

Page 63: Bill Watterson, *Calvin and Hobbes*, 1993.

Page 64: Jackie Ormes, *Patty-Jo 'n' Ginger*, 1956.

Page 65: Nell Brinkley, *Kathleen and the Great Secret*, 1920.

Page 66: Marge (Marjorie Henderson Buell), *Little Lulu*, 1940.

Page 67: Scott Adams, *Dilbert*, c. 2000.

Page 68: Richard F. Outcault, *The Yellow Kid (McFadden's Row of Flats)*, 1896.

Page 69: Dav Pilkey, *Dog Man*, 2016.

Page 70: Harvey Kurtzman, *Hey Look!*, 1949.

Page 71: Rube Goldberg, *The Inventions of Professor Lucifer G. Butts, A.K.*, 1931.

Page 72: Scott McCloud, *Understanding Comics*, 1993.

Page 73: Art Spiegelman, *Maus*, c. 1986.

Page 74: Gary Panter, *Jimbo*, 1980.

Page 75: Chris Ware, *Quimby the Mouse*, c. 1997.

Page 76: Harvey Pekar and Gerry Shamray, *American Splendor*, c. 1987.

Page 77: Charles M. Schulz, *Peanuts*, c. 1967.

Page 78: Herb Trimpe and Bob McLeod, *G.I. Joe*, 1982.

Page 79: Milton Caniff, *Steve Canyon*, c. 1954.

Page 80: Aaron McGruder, *The Boondocks*, 2000.

Page 81: Dale Messick, *Brenda Starr, Reporter*, c. 1960.

Page 82: Walt Kelly, *Pogo*, c. 1955.

Page 83: Roz Chast, *Going Into Town*, 2017.

Page 84: Frank Miller, *Sin City*, c. 1994.

Page 85: R. Crumb, *Fritz the Cat*, 1968.

Page 86: Jack Kirby and Joe Sinnott, *Fantastic Four*, 1969.

Page 87: Bianca Xunise, *Six Chix*, 2020.

Page 88: Kazu Kibuishi, *Amulet*, c. 2009.

Page 89: Matt Baker, *Phantom Lady*, 1948.

Page 90: Jacob Chabot, *Spongebob Comics*, 2015.

Page 91: Sarah Andersen, *Sarah's Scribbles*, 2016.

Page 92: Rudolph Dirks, *The Katzenjammer Kids*, c. 1907.

Page 93: Billy Graham, *Luke Cage, Hero For Hire*, 1973.

Page 94: Jamie McKelvie and Matt Wilson, *Ms. Marvel*, 2014.

Page 95: Ernie Bushmiller, *Nancy*, c. 1970.

Page 96: Ty Templeton, *Batman & Robin Adventures*, 1995.

Page 97: Jim Steranko, *The Incredible Hulk*, 1968.

Page 98: Howard Cruse, *Wendel*, c. 1988.

Page 99: Gustave Verbeek, *The Upside Downs of Little Lady Lovekins and Old Man Muffaroo*, c. 1905.

Page 100: Jim Davis, *Garfield*, c. 1995.

Page 101: Crockett Johnson, *Barnaby*, 1943.

Page 102: Jason Ho, Mike Rote, and Nathan Kane, *Simpsons Comics*, 2014.

Page 103: H. G. Peter, *Wonder Woman*, c. 1945.

Page 104: Ralph Heimdahl and Fred Abranz, *Bugs Bunny* and *Daffy Duck*, c. 1960.

Page 105: Ernie Colón, *Richie Rich and Casper*, 1977.

Page 106: Warren Tufts, *Scooby Doo… Where Are You!*, 1971.

Page 107: Stephan Pastis, *Pearls Before Swine*, 2012.

Page 108: Luke McDonnell, Ian Akin, and Brian Garvey, *Iron Man*, 1985.

Page 109: Jerry Scott and Jim Borgman, *Zits*, 2006.

Page 110: Rebecca Sugar, *Steven Universe*, 2014.

Page 111: Barbara Brandon-Croft, *Where I'm Coming From*, c. 1994.

Page 112: Steve Ditko, *Dr. Strange*, c. 1965.

Page 113: Al Capp, *Li'l Abner*, c. 1955.

Page 114: Neal Adams, *Green Lantern*, 1971.

Page 115: Gene Hazelton, *The Flintstones*, c. 1970.

Page 116: Paul Smith, *The Uncanny X-Men*, 1983.

Page 117: Noelle Stevenson, *Lumberjanes*, 2014.

Page 118: Gene Luen Yang, *Boxers & Saints*, 2013.

Every effort has been made to identify the artists and details listed here. Please contact the publisher if there are any errors.

Notes

Portions of the Constitution and the Amendments have been revised or repealed by later Amendments.

Page 9: *"Representatives and direct Taxes shall be apportioned among the several States which may be included within this Union, according to their respective Numbers, which shall be determined by adding to the whole Number of free Persons, including those bound to Service for a Term of Years, and excluding Indians not taxed, three fifths of all other Persons."* From Article I, Section 2, this has been changed by Amendment XIV, Section 2 **(page 95)**. The apportionment of taxes has been changed by Amendment XVI **(page 99)**.

Page 12: *"chosen by the Legislature thereof"* From Article I, Section 3, this has been revised by Amendment XVII **(page 100)**.

Page 13: *"and if Vacancies happen by Resignation, or otherwise, during the Recess of the Legislature of any State, the Executive thereof may make temporary Appointments until the next Meeting of the Legislature, which shall then fill such Vacancies."* From Article I, Section 3, this has been revised by Amendment XVII **(page 101)**.

Page 16: *"and such Meeting shall be on the first Monday in December"* From Article I, Section 4, this has been changed by Amendment XX, Section 2 **(page 104)**.

Page 33: *"unless in Proportion to the Census or Enumeration herein before directed to be taken."* From Article I, Section 9, this has been affected by Amendment XVI **(page 99)**.

Pages 41–43: *"The Electors shall meet in their respective States, and vote by Ballot for two Persons, of whom one at least shall not be an Inhabitant of the same State with themselves. And they shall make a List of all the Persons voted for, and of the Number of Votes for each; which List they shall sign and certify, and transmit sealed to the Seat of the Government of the United States, directed to the President of the Senate. The President of the Senate shall, in the Presence of the Senate and House of Representatives, open all the Certificates, and the Votes shall then be counted. The Person having the greatest Number of Votes shall be the President, if such Number be a Majority of the whole Number of Electors appointed;*

and if there be more than one who have such Majority, and have an equal Number of Votes, then the House of Representatives shall immediately chuse by Ballot one of them for President; and if no Person have a

Majority, then from the five highest on the List the said House shall in like Manner chuse the President. But in chusing the President, the Votes shall be taken by States, the Representation from each State having one Vote; A quorum for this Purpose shall consist of a Member or Members from two thirds of the States, and a Majority of all the States shall be necessary to a Choice. In every Case, after the Choice of the President, the Person having the greatest Number of Votes of the Electors shall be the Vice President. But if there should remain two or more who have equal Votes, the Senate shall chuse from them by Ballot the Vice President." From Article II, Section 1, this entire clause has been superseded by Amendment XII **(pages 89–92)**.

Page 45: "*In Case of the Removal of the President from Office, or of his Death, Resignation, or Inability to discharge the Powers and Duties of the said Office, the Same shall devolve on the Vice President, and the Congress may by Law provide for the Case of Removal, Death, Resignation or Inability, both of the President and Vice President, declaring what Officer shall then act as President, and such Officer shall act accordingly, until the Disability be removed, or a President shall be elected.*" From Article II, Section 1, this has been changed by Amendment XXV **(pages 112–116)**.

Page 54: "*between a State and Citizens of another State*" and "*and between a State, or the Citizens thereof, and foreign States, Citizens or Subjects.*" From Article III, Section 2, these have been changed by Amendment XI **(page 88)**.

Page 59: "*No Person held to Service or Labour in one State, under the Laws thereof, escaping into another, shall, in Consequence of any Law or Regulation therein, be discharged from such Service or Labour, but shall be delivered up on Claim of the Party to whom such Service or Labour may be due.*" From Article IV, Section 2, this clause has been superseded by Amendment XIII **(page 93)**.

Page 91: "*And if the House of Representatives shall not choose a President whenever the right of choice shall devolve upon them, before the fourth day of March next following, then the Vice-President shall act as President, as in the case of the death or other constitutional disability of the President.--*" From Amendment XII, this has been superseded by Amendment XX, Section 3 **(page 105)**.

Page 95: "*being twenty-one years of age,*" From Amendment XIV, Section 2, this has been changed by Amendment XXVI, Section 1 **(page 117)**.

Page 102: Amendment XVIII was repealed by Amendment XXI, Section 1 **(page 107)**.

Chronology

The Constitutional Convention of the states opened in Philadelphia on **May 25, 1787,** to revise their Articles of Confederation. Over that summer, the delegates developed the **Constitution** (pages 5–69).

The Constitution was signed by the delegates of 12 states on **September 17, 1787,** and it was sent to the state conventions for ratification (pages 70–72).

The Constitution became effective on **June 21, 1788,** once nine states had ratified it. The remaining four states followed over the next two years. The last of the original 13 states, Rhode Island, ratified it on **May 29, 1790.**

The first U.S. Congress met in New York City on **March 4, 1789.** The Congress proposed 12 amendments to the Constitution on **September 25, 1789** (pages 74–76).

Ten of those 12 amendments, known as **The Bill of Rights,** were ratified by the states on **December 15, 1791** (pages 77–86).

Amendments XI–XXVII were ratified between **1795** and **1992** (pages 88–118).

Amendment XI was proposed on **March 4, 1794** and ratified on **February 7, 1795.**

Amendment XII was proposed on **December 9, 1803** and ratified on **June 15, 1804.**

Amendment XIII was proposed on **January 31, 1865** and ratified on **December 6, 1865.**

Amendment XIV was proposed on **June 13, 1866** and ratified on **July 9, 1868.**

Amendment XV was proposed on **February 26, 1869** and ratified on **February 3, 1870.**

Amendment XVI was proposed on **July 12, 1909** and ratified on **February 3, 1913.**

Amendment XVII was proposed on **May 13, 1912** and ratified on **April 8, 1913.**

Amendment XVIII was proposed on **December 18, 1917** and ratified on **January 16, 1919.**

Amendment XIX was proposed on **June 4, 1919** and ratified on **August 18, 1920.**

Amendment XX was proposed on **March 2, 1932** and ratified on **January 23, 1933.**

Amendment **XXI** was proposed on **February 20, 1933** and ratified on **December 5, 1933.**

Amendment **XXII** was proposed on **March 21, 1947** and ratified on **February 27, 1951.**

Amendment **XXIII** was proposed on **June 16, 1960** and ratified on **March 29, 1961.**

Amendment **XXIV** was proposed on **August 27, 1962** and ratified on **January 23, 1964.**

Amendment **XXV** was proposed on **July 6, 1965** and ratified on **February 10, 1967.**

Amendment **XXVI** was proposed on **March 23, 1971** and ratified on **July 1, 1971.**

Amendment **XXVII** was one of the first 12 amendments proposed on **September 25, 1789,** and it was finally ratified on **May 7, 1992.**

Selected Bibliography

Arnold, Andrew B. *A Pocket Guide to the US Constitution.* Georgetown University Press, 2018.

"The Bill of Rights: A Transcription." *National Archives and Records Administration*, www.archives.gov/ founding-docs/bill-of-rights-transcript.

"The Constitution of the United States: A Transcription." *National Archives and Records Administration*, www.archives. gov/founding-docs/constitution-transcript.

"The Constitution: Amendments 11–27." *National Archives and Records Administration*, www.archives.gov/ founding-docs/amendments-11-27.

Fink, Sam. *The Constitution of the United States of America: With Benjamin Franklin's Address to the Delegates Upon the Signing of the Constitution.* Welcome Books, 2006.

"Interactive Constitution: The National Constitution Center." *Interactive Constitution | The National Constitution Center*, www.constitutioncenter.org/ interactive-constitution.

"Resolution of the Federal Convention Submitting the Constitution to Congress, September 17, 1787." *Avalon Project*, www.avalon.law.yale.edu/18th_century/ ressub01.asp.

R. Sikoryak is the author of *Masterpiece Comics, Terms and Conditions,* and *The Unquotable Trump.* His illustrations and comics have appeared in *The New Yorker, The New York Times Book Review, The Nation, MAD,* and many other publications. He also hosts the comics performance series Carousel, and he teaches at Parsons School of Design. Sikoryak lives in New York City with his spouse Kriota Willberg.